TIMEF

HORSES TO ᴍᴜᴌᴌᴜ

2022/23 JUMPS SEASON

CONTENTS

TIMEFORM

ISBN 978-1-8380349-4-8 Price £10.95

Printed and bound by
Charlesworth Press,
Wakefield, UK 01924 204830

SECTION

Timeform's Fifty To Follow, carefully chosen by members of Timeform's editorial staff, are listed below with their respective page numbers. A selection of ten (marked in bold with a ★) is made for those who prefer a smaller list.

The form summary for each horse is shown after its age, colour, sex and pedigree. The summary shows the distance, the state of the going and where the horse finished in each of its races since the start of the 2021/22 season. Performances are in chronological sequence with the date of its last race shown at the end (F-ran on Flat).

The distance of each race is given in furlongs. Steeplechase form figures are prefixed by the letter 'c', hurdle form figures by the letter 'h' and NH Flat race or bumper form figures by the letter 'b'.

The going is symbolised as follows: f–firm, m–good to firm; g–good, d–good to soft; s–soft; v–heavy.

Placings are indicated, up to the sixth place, by use of superior figures, an asterisk being used to denote a win and superior letters are used to convey what happened to a horse during the race: F–fell, pu–pulled up, ur–unseated rider, bd–brought down, su–slipped up, ro–ran out.

The Timeform Rating of a horse is simply the merit of the horse expressed in pounds and is arrived at by careful examination of its running against other horses. The ratings range from 175+ for the champions down to a figure of around 55 for selling platers. Symbols attached to the ratings: 'p'–likely to improve; 'P'–capable of much better form; '+'–the horse may be better than we have rated it.

Ahoy Senor (Ire)   c161p

7 b.g. Dylan Thomas (Ire) – Dara Supreme (Ire) (Darazari (Ire))

2021/22 c20s^{ur} c23.4d* c24s^2 c24.2d* c24.4s^2 c25g* Apr 8

It was at the 2021 Grand National meeting that Ahoy Senor first made a name for himself, making all the running to win the Grade 1 Sefton Novices' Hurdle on just his second start over hurdles at odds of 66/1. He did better still over fences last season, finishing up with another Grade 1 success back at Aintree in the spring in the Mildmay Novices' Chase. Ahoy Senor beat the outsider of the quartet in the Mildmay, Fury Road, by five lengths, after again leading throughout, whereas neither of the first two in the betting, L'Homme Presse and Bravemansgame, gave their running. The same pair were the only ones who'd beaten Ahoy Senor earlier in the season.

But those disappointing efforts from his main rivals doesn't detract from a high-class performance from Ahoy Senor, who had excuses for both his earlier defeats. When he was beaten by Bravemansgame—who'd finished second to him in the Sefton, incidentally—in the Kauto Star Novices' Chase at Kempton, Ahoy Senor failed to make it enough of a test of stamina which left him vulnerable to a rival who was more the finished article and had a bit more pace. It was jumping that was a decisive factor in Ahoy Senor's defeat to L'Homme Presse in the Brown Advisory Novices' Chase at Cheltenham where, in contrast

Ahoy Senor looks a top-class staying chaser in the making

to the winner, Ahoy Senor was less assured in that department, a mistake at a key stage of the race three out an important one.

Ahoy Senor failed to complete when highly tried on his chasing debut in the Colin Parker Memorial Intermediate Chase at Carlisle, though he jumped accurately until unlucky to stumble and unseat two out. But his two other wins during the season prior to Aintree were impressive ones in Grade 2 company, coming home a long way clear of his three rivals in the John Francome Novices' Chase at Newbury in November and jumping boldly on the way to beating the subsequent Grand National winner Noble Yeats with plenty in hand, giving him 5 lb, in the Towton Novices' Chase at Wetherby in February.

Ahoy Senor is a big, raw-boned gelding, with the overall impression he gave in his novice season being that he's not yet the finished article. That's despite proving himself one of the season's best novices in Britain, which makes him such an exciting prospect for all the top staying chases. His latest win at Aintree came on good ground, having raced only on softer going previously, and he acts on heavy. ***Lucinda Russell***

Conclusion: *Showed plenty of raw talent in his first season over fences but strongly hinted that there's better still to come and capable of winning a big staying prize*

Aucunrisque (Fr) h138

6 b.g. No Risk At All (Fr) – Saintheze (Fr) (Saint des Saints (Fr))
2021/22 b16.3g* b16.4m⁴ b16.4g³ h15.9d² h15.9s* h15.2d* h16d* h16.5g⁴
h15.9g* Apr 17

Chris Gordon will be hoping that Aucunrisque's novice chasing campaign pans out better than that of Highway One O Two, who preceded his stable companion by winning the 2020 edition of the Grade 2 Dovecote Novices' Hurdle at Kempton but then made a disastrous start to life over fences the following season. He first suffered a heavy fall at Ffos Las and then unseated his rider at Carlisle before Gordon made the decision to draw stumps and revert to hurdling. It wasn't until December last season that Highway One O Two finally regained the winning thread in a handicap hurdle at Taunton, but it will be a surprise if Aucunrisque isn't capable of winning more races in the short term such was the impression he created in his first full season of racing under Rules.

Lightly raced in points before joining Gordon, Aucunrisque filled the runner-up spot in a Stratford bumper in March 2021 and then reappeared after six months off with a pillar-to-post victory in a similar event over the same course and distance. He failed to add to his tally in two subsequent starts in bumpers but showed even better form in defeat both times, notably finishing third, beaten just a length and a half, in a listed contest at Cheltenham's November Meeting where his failure to settle probably cost him his chance.

Aucunrisque (black cap) won four of his six starts over hurdles last season

After losing out by a nose on his hurdling debut at Plumpton in December—a novice won by Highway One O Two in 2019 and another stablemate, Annual Invictus, in 2020—Aucunrisque then rattled off three straight wins in a novice hurdle back at Plumpton, a novice handicap hurdle at Wincanton and, of course, the Dovecote at Kempton. There was plenty to like about his attitude on the last occasion, moving to the front at the fourth flight and finding plenty after being joined at the last to land the spoils by a length.

That was a useful performance and Aucunrisque ran to a similar level when also winning a handicap hurdle back at Plumpton in April, that coming only nine days after he had finished a well-held fourth in the Top Novices' Hurdle at Aintree. He defied a BHA mark of 133 at Plumpton and once again showed an outstanding attitude, rallying bravely after being headed on the home turn to get the verdict by a nose.

Now up to a BHA mark of 137 over hurdles, the tough Aucunrisque is reportedly all set to embark on a chasing career this term and his style of racing (front runner/races prominently) should lend itself well to that sphere. He raced exclusively at around two miles last season but should stay further, with novice handicaps at up to two and a half miles likely to be on the agenda. ***Chris Gordon***

Conclusion: *Likeable sort who improved in leaps and bounds over hurdles last season and has the potential to go on again over fences; will stay 2½m*

Ballygrifincottage (Ire) h135

7 b.g. Stowaway – Long Long Time (Ire) (Dr Massini (Ire))
2021/22 h24g³ h23s* h24d⁴ Mar 18

Having won all three completed starts in Irish points, it came as little surprise that the Dan Skelton team harboured high hopes for Ballygrifincottage last season. By Stowaway out of a winning pointer, he was thrown in at the deep end by his new connections at Cheltenham in December where the Grade 2 Albert Bartlett Novices' Hurdle was the chosen race for his debut under Rules, a contest which attracted a strong field headed by eventual winner Blazing Khal and fellow *Fifty* member Gelino Bello.

Ballygrifincottage was sent off a relatively unconsidered 22/1 chance but shaped far better than those odds might suggest. Waited with in the early stages, he wasn't fluent at the first or second but settled into a rhythm from there. He made good headway to hold every chance between the last two hurdles but was unable to quicken on the uphill climb to the line, eventually passing the post six lengths behind the winner in third.

All in all, it was an encouraging start to his career and Ballygrifincottage didn't need to improve on that form to get off the mark under Rules in a novice hurdle at the valuable Winter Millions fixture at Lingfield the following month. He was again settled in rear early on before making steady headway to be in contention two out. Under pressure before the final flight, he responded generously and was well on top at the finish, ultimately beating High Stakes by a length and a half.

That was enough to book his place at the Cheltenham Festival where he proved to be the best of the British in finishing fourth (beaten 13 lengths) behind The Nice Guy in the Albert Bartlett Novices' Hurdle. The emphasis on stamina seemed to suit as he made good progress to chase the leaders before the last having seemingly been labouring and in trouble three out.

A big, raw-boned type, Ballygrifincottage is more of a chaser than a hurdler on looks and is entitled to improve for a switch to fences this season. He's clearly in very good hands and, having already shown a useful level of form over timber—while being lightly raced—it will be interesting to see how far he can go this term. *Dan Skelton*

Conclusion: *Ran well for one so inexperienced when fourth in the Albert Bartlett at the Cheltenham Festival and looks a sure-fire improver in novice chases over 3m+*

Beauport (Ire)   h149

6 b.g. Califet (Fr) – Byerley Beauty (Ire) (Brian Boru)
2021/22 h19.8s² h20.5s² h23.5d² h20s* h24.7d⁴ Apr 9

Beauport had looked like a promising young horse when ploughing through the mud to win the EBF Final in March 2021, though conditions at Sandown that afternoon were so extreme there was an obvious question about whether he was flattered in a race where many failed to handle the ground. His efforts last season, however, show that he is not simply a mudlark and that his EBF Final success owed more to his huge engine than it did the frailties of his rivals.

Beauport may have won only one of his five starts last season, but he shaped really well on the four occasions he met with defeat, never finishing outside the frame, and ended the campaign with a Timeform rating 18 lb higher than it had been prior to his return at Sandown in November.

Beauport was an encouraging second on that reappearance and he backed up that positive impression when filling the same position at Newbury on his next outing, faring best of those who had been held up. The way Beauport shaped at Newbury suggested that he would benefit from a stiffer test of stamina and he proved as much on his first crack at a trip around three miles at Sandown in February, despite again having to settle for second in a good-quality contest.

A string of seconds can sometimes lead to questions over a horse's resolution, but that was never really the case with Beauport, who was showing progressive form but simply had the misfortune of bumping into well-handicapped rivals. Beauport snapped the sequence of seconds, however, when gaining a deserved win in a two-and-a-half-mile handicap hurdle at Uttoxeter in March, displaying a teak-tough attitude to get the better of the unexposed favourite, with the pair drawing 15 lengths clear in a pulsating battle.

Significant interference prevented Beauport from building on that form when only fourth on his final start at Aintree, but he would have finished much closer had he not been shuffled right back on the home turn when going strongly, costing him as many as 10 lengths. The way he rallied up the home straight, passing a host of rivals, underlined his likeable attitude and he has the attributes required to make up into a smashing novice chaser. **Nigel Twiston-Davies**

Conclusion: *Showed gradual improvement in really competitive handicap hurdles last season, impressing with his attitude and looking like a strong stayer; his physique and straightforward nature suggest he will take well to chasing*

Black Poppy   h121

6 b.g. Kayf Tara – Poppy Come Running (Ire) (Definite Article)
2021/22 h16.7d^F h16s^3 h15.8g^4 h16s^2 h16.2d* h16.3s* h16.3g^2 Apr 1

Black Poppy had sprung a 25/1 surprise when successful on his only bumper start in the spring of 2021, but he was a much shorter price for his hurdling debut at Bangor last season and was in the process of running well, looking all set to finish a clear second, when falling two out. It took Black Poppy a few runs to confirm the promise of that first effort, but he eventually did so at Kempton on Boxing Day, albeit proving no match for the odds-on Nicky Henderson-trained winner Broomfield Burg, who beat him 10 lengths after Black Poppy took a keen hold early on before keeping on to take second late on.

But it wasn't until going handicapping after the turn of the year that Black Poppy's season began to gather momentum. He started at a shade of odds on for his handicap debut in a novice contest at Hereford in January and showed a really likeable attitude to emerge the winner by a neck from Just The Man after being headed briefly on the run-in and then rallying to edge ahead again near the line. He had even less to spare in another steadily-run contest at Newbury in March when again strong in the betting. After travelling well and looming up in the straight to lead two out, Black Poppy had to work harder when strongly pressed on the run-in for a short-head verdict over Straw Fan Jack.

On his final start of the season, back at Newbury, Black Poppy was involved in his third tight finish, but this time he came off second best in going down by a nose to fellow novice Mark of Gold. Once again, however, Black Poppy showed good battling qualities once headed at the last, rallying on the run-in and was in front again a stride after the line. Out of a bumper winner from the family of triple Champion Hurdle winner Istabraq, no less, Black Poppy has raced only at around two miles, but he can be expected to stay further and acts on soft ground. He's not the biggest but should do at least as well over fences. **Kerry Lee**

Conclusion: *Showed a good attitude in some close finishes to win a couple of handicap hurdles and set for further success in similar company over fences*

Blue Beach   b107

5 b.m. Kayf Tara – Flutter Bye (Ire) (Alflora (Ire))
2021/22 b15.8s* Mar 29

The flagship horse for Mel Rowley's Bridgnorth yard last term was the useful chaser Wishing And Hoping, a former hunter who, despite turning 12 during the season, acquitted himself well in handicaps, winning a veterans' race at Aintree in the autumn, finishing placed behind younger rivals in some decent races at Kempton and Warwick and competing at both Cheltenham and Aintree in the spring. But the stable's wishes and hopes for the future almost certainly lie with the five-year-old mare Blue Beach, who was a convincing winner of a bumper at Uttoxeter in March on her only start.

The likes of Nicky Henderson, Alan King and Nigel Twiston-Davies had some of the better-fancied mares in the line-up, with Henderson's runner Touchy Feely sent off the 11/8 favourite on the strength of her encouraging second on her debut in a similar event at Newbury earlier in the month. Blue Beach was among the outsiders at 40/1 but belied her odds, not only upsetting the better-fancied horses but doing so in the manner of a potentially useful type. Ridden handily throughout, she was produced to lead with three furlongs to run and showed an impressive to turn of foot in the soft ground to draw clear, spread-eagling the field behind her. The King-trained newcomer Passing Reflection was a dozen lengths back in second ahead of the favourite, with the remainder well strung out.

A daughter of Kayf Tara, Blue Beach is closely related to Pique Rock, a winning pointer for Mel Rowley's husband Phil and later a fairly useful chaser for Henry Daly. Their dam was only modest over hurdles but was a half-sister to I'msingingtheblues, a smart chaser at short of three miles, firstly for Paul Nicholls and then David Pipe. Blue Beach looks the type to win more races, probably in mares' novice hurdles, and the way she won her bumper suggests she could prove useful. *Mel Rowley*

Conclusion: *Belied long odds when spread-eagling the field in a mares' bumper on her only start and could be a useful novice in mares' contests over hurdles*

Call of The Wild (Ire)   h126

5 b.g. Fame And Glory – Glory Days (Ger) (Tiger Hill (Ire))
2021/22 b15.8d* h16.3d² h16g* h16.6v* h20.3g³ Apr 13

Call of The Wild is bred more for speed than stamina, being out of a daughter of Fillies' Mile winner Glorosia, and a key feature of his performances during his first campaign over hurdles was how strongly he travelled.

Call of The Wild proved far too sharp for his rivals on his sole start in bumpers at Huntingdon last May, quickening eight and a half lengths clear, and he made a promising start to his hurdling career at Stratford nearly six months later when a final-flight blunder meant he had to settle for second behind a rival with much more experience to call on. The winner, Onemorefortheroad, subsequently landed handicaps at Huntingdon and Newbury before hitting the frame in the Betfair Exchange Trophy, Imperial Cup and Scottish Champion Hurdle, so it reflects really well on Call of The Wild that he left the impression he should have won at Stratford, even if he was in receipt of 11 lb.

Given the promise Call of The Wild showed at Stratford, he made rather heavy weather of landing the odds in a three-runner novice at Kempton a few weeks later, but he was much more impressive when defying a penalty at Doncaster on his return from a three-month break. They went a steady pace in that Doncaster novice, so it was impressive how much distance Call of The Wild and runner-up Boombawn managed to put between themselves and the other two runners, with Call of The Wild ultimately asserting in ready fashion to score by four and a quarter lengths.

Call of The Wild failed to show the same sort of form when last seen finishing third in a novice hurdle at Cheltenham in April (after which he was treated for heat stress), but the step up to two and a half miles at a stiff track probably didn't suit such a pacy sort and he is likely to be seen to better effect when there's a greater emphasis on speed. It's worth noting that the form of his Doncaster victory was franked by Boombawn winning two novice hurdles before finishing runner-up in the Novices' Championship Final at Sandown, and Call of The Wild will be one to note when tackling handicaps. *Alan King*

Conclusion: *Has some strong novice form to his name and looks tailormade for 2m handicaps in which he can utilise his high cruising speed; versatile regards ground conditions but likely to be at his very best when the emphasis is on speed*

 # Complete Unknown (Ire) h132

6 b.g. Dylan Thomas (Ire) – Silver Stream (Ire) (Milan)
2021/22 h19d³ h19.5d² h21.6d³ h21.6s² h19.8s* h23.9s² Apr 20

The EBF 'National Hunt' Novices' Handicap Hurdle Final at Sandown in March is often worth more than one watch with the race having thrown up plenty of household names over the years. Alberta's Run is perhaps the best winner of the race in recent times—he emerged victorious in 2007 before going on to record back-to-back wins in the Ryanair Chase in 2010 and 2011—while The Listener, Dynaste, Many Clouds and Whisper all feature among those to have come up short in the race before going on to show top-class form when switched to fences.

Only time will tell whether last year's winner Complete Unknown can do likewise, but he is certainly a promising recruit to the novice chasing ranks this season. After winning his sole start in bumpers at Thurles in March 2021 when trained by Jonathan Fogarty, Complete Unknown was then bought for £115,000 and joined Paul Nicholls. Further success for his new stable didn't immediately come his way and he met with defeat in his first four starts over hurdles. However, he still achieved a useful level of form, notably

Complete Unknown showed improved form to get off the mark at Sandown

passing the post less than four lengths behind the winner, Party Business, when third in what proved to be a strong maiden hurdle at Ascot in December.

Complete Unknown promised to have an even bigger effort in the locker when everything fell right and so it proved when he made his handicap debut at Sandown. Lining up there from a BHA mark of 126, he looked in great shape beforehand and clearly relished the soft going as he showed improved form to get off the mark over hurdles. Waited with in the early stages, he travelled smoothly and quickened to lead soon after two out, always doing enough from there to win by three lengths in comfortable fashion.

Though unable to follow up on his final outing in a listed novice hurdle at Perth in April, Complete Unknown ran at least as well in defeat there as when winning at Sandown, sticking to his task well to be beaten only two and a quarter lengths behind Mahler Mission. That effort proved his stamina for three miles—two and three-quarter miles was the furthest he'd gone prior to that—and everything about him suggests he has the makings of a smart staying novice chaser this season. A tall gelding, he is certainly bred to stay well as his unraced dam is closely related to the Betfair Chase winner Snoopy Loopy. **Paul Nicholls**

Conclusion: *Developed into a useful novice hurdler last season but was essentially just biding his time before going over fences this season; looks a smart prospect for novice chases at up to 3m*

Dusart (Ire) c151

7 b.g. Flemensfirth (USA) – Dusty Too (Terimon)
2021/22 c22.7d* c24.2d* c24.4s⁵ c24.1g* Apr 2

Nicky Henderson won three editions of the Hennessy Gold Cup with Trabolgan, Bobs Worth and Triolo d'Alene, the last of those in 2013. The closest he went to winning any of the five editions run under the Ladbrokes Trophy banner was with Whisper in 2017, but this season Henderson could well have an ideal type for the Newbury race now called the Coral Gold Cup.

Newbury was where Dusart made his debut over hurdles in the autumn of 2020 and he looked a star in the making when beating the subsequent Betfair Hurdle winner Soaring Glory. But injury kept off him off the track for most of that season and he managed only one more run over hurdles, running well despite his obvious inexperience to finish third in the Top Novices' Hurdle at Aintree.

While those two runs over hurdles were both over two miles, he's essentially a staying type and was stepped up markedly in trip for his novice chase campaign which began with easy wins in small fields at Leicester and Exeter. A tendency to jump left was evident in both those wins and, after that gentle introduction to chasing, his inexperience showed when he took on some of the top staying novices in the Brown Advisory Novices' Chase at the Cheltenham Festival. But after a bad mistake at the twelfth, he finished quite well up the hill for a never-dangerous fifth behind L'Homme Presse.

That gave Dusart a BHA mark of 147 for his first start in a handicap which came in a good-quality novice contest on the Scottish National card at Ayr. Jumping better this time, Dusart had to work hard but ultimately rallied to see off the challenge of fellow *Fifty* member Sounds Russian and win by half a length under top weight. With just six starts all told, the well-made Dusart is still something of a work in progress but that bodes well considering his form is already smart. He's a half-brother to the top-class chaser Simonsig, who represented the same connections, but he's more of a stayer than that horse and, given that he'll stay beyond three miles, the Coral Gold Cup looks a perfect target for him. ***Nicky Henderson***

Conclusion: *Confirmed previous season's promise over hurdles when winning three of his four chase starts and has the potential to do better still over fences, starting with the Coral Gold Cup*

East Street (Ire) h112

6 b.g. Mores Wells – Serpentine Mine (Ire) (Rashar (USA))
2021/22 h16d* h16.2g² h19.3s h18.9m³ h20.1d* Apr 11

Trevor Hemmings, one of jump racing's most popular and successful owners, died in October 2021 at the age of 86. He won the Grand National three times with Hedgehunter,

Ballabriggs and Many Clouds, just some of the many good staying chasers to carry the yellow and green quartered colours with white sleeves and cap. Others included the high-class The Last Fling, who won several of Haydock's valuable chases, and Vintage Clouds, who was Hemmings' last big winner when successful in the 2021 Ultima Handicap Chase at the Cheltenham Festival.

The latter pair were trained by Sue Smith, who looks to have another future staying chaser on her hands in the Hemmings' colours, which live on, in the form of East Street. He'd finished runner-up on the second of a couple of starts in Irish points before making a successful Rules debut in a two-mile novice hurdle at Wetherby in November. East Street made all the running, giving the firm impression that longer trips would bring out the best in him.

East Street proved no match for Since Day One at Newcastle kept to two miles next time and was then stepped up in distance for his last three starts in handicaps. He was badly hampered early on in the first of those at Catterick, and then kept on for third behind Hurricane Ali at Haydock next time where the extended two and a quarter mile trip on firmish ground still looked an inadequate test. But it was a different story on his final outing of the season at Hexham in April where East Street relished the combination of two and a half miles over that stiff track and softer going. Having taken a keen hold, East Street went on two out and was clear early in the straight. Tackled at the last, he then found extra to win by a length and three-quarters from Foster'sisland, justifying some solid support in the process.

From the family of those smart chasers Spiritofthegames and Acting Lass, East Street will be suited by three miles when he goes over fences and it would be no surprise to see him better the fair form he showed over hurdles last term. **Sue Smith**

Conclusion: *Ex-pointer who ran his best race over hurdles given his stiffest test of stamina to date on his final start and looks another staying chaser in the making in his late owner's colours*

Fenland Tiger   h78p
6 ch.g. Schiaparelli (Ger) – La Calinda (Presenting)
2021/22 b15.8d b16.2g h15.7d³ h16s h16d Jan 27

Mention the West Yorkshire town of Guiseley and the first thing that's likely to come to mind for many is Harry Ramsden's 'world famous' fish and chip shop. But it's also the location of Sam England's stable which had its best campaign yet in 2021/22 with 19 winners. That total could be under threat this season as the yard is already nearly halfway to matching that total at the time of writing.

One who should be contributing to his stable's tally this season is Fenland Tiger, though at first glance his form so far might suggest that's unlikely. But Fenland Tiger has done all his racing over two miles whilst shaping as though the best of him won't be seen until he tackles much longer distances. He gave that impression initially in a couple of bumpers at Uttoxeter and Newcastle before the turn of the year, finishing mid-division at best, and then had three runs over hurdles in January.

Fenland Tiger made late headway to finish a remote third to the fairly useful pair Socialist Agenda and Malpas in a five-runner novice at Catterick on New Year's Day and was beaten a long way again at Wetherby on his last two outings, on the final one again closing up late having been well off the pace. Those modest efforts will mean that Fenland Tiger goes into handicaps with a lot of untapped potential, something a step up in trip should help him realise. A switch to fences at some stage is likely to be beneficial, too, as he's a chasing type on looks.

Fenland Tiger's pedigree also suggests stamina will prove his forte as he's by Schiaparelli, whose wins included the Goodwood Cup, and a half-brother to Teescomponentstrig, a fair three-mile hurdle winner, while his grandam Bayrouge was a useful hurdler/chaser who won at up to 25 furlongs. *Sam England*

Conclusion: *Showed just modest form in a handful of starts in bumpers/over hurdles but shaped like a stayer and capable of exploiting his lowly mark in handicaps given a sufficient test*

Findthetime (Ire)   h124p

6 b.g. Shantou (USA) – Bisoguet (Ire) (Definite Article)
2021/22 h16.2d³ h17.1m² h16.8d* h19.3s* h19.7v* Feb 16

Findthetime improved in leaps and bounds over hurdles last season, rattling off a hat-trick, and there is the potential for even better to come given his lightly raced profile and the sharp upward trajectory he is tracking.

Findthetime was easy to back and shaped as if better for the run when making his Rules debut in a novice hurdle at Perth last September, ultimately finishing a well-beaten third. He then lined up over a slightly longer trip at Carlisle the following month where, despite still looking very raw, he showed improved form to fill the runner-up spot, passing the post five and a half lengths behind the winner. He stayed on in encouraging style, shaping like one who would benefit from going further still, so it was to his credit that he was then able to get off the mark in a similar contest at Sedgefield that placed a greater emphasis on speed than ideal.

It was little surprise to see Findthetime upped in trip for his handicap debut at Catterick in December and he duly took another step forward to land that 19-furlong affair, staying on strongly to assert in the final 100 yards of a race which had been run at a good gallop. The going was soft at Catterick, but Timeform described conditions as being even more testing at Wetherby in February when Findthetime stepped up in grade to contest a good-quality handicap over just shy of two and a half miles. He seemed to relish conditions, though, and once again proved strong at the finish as he drew six and a half lengths clear, leaving the impression he ought to stay further.

There are more races to be won over hurdles with Findthetime if connections decide to stick to that discipline for a bit longer, while chasing is also an option for this ex-pointer who held every chance when falling at the final fence on his only start between the flags.

Nicky Richards

Conclusion: *Ex-pointer who progressed well over hurdles last season and still has more to offer, with a step up in trip promising to unlock further improvement*

Fontaine Collonges (Fr)   c134
7 b.m. Saddler Maker (Ire) – Saturne Collonges (Fr) (Dom Alco (Fr))
2021/22 c15.2d⁴ c20g* c20.6g⁴ c20s* Jan 21

There was a valuable new addition to the jumping calendar last season with the inaugural Winter Million meeting taking place at Lingfield in January. The second day of the three-day fixture was an all-weather Flat card, but the other two days featured some valuable contests over jumps, including the Fleur de Lys Chase, a two-mile six-furlong contest worth almost £80,000 to the winner which drew some smart performers and had an exciting finish with Two For Gold getting the better of Dashel Drasher and Bristol de Mai.

The first day of the meeting was a good one for Venetia Williams, who had a double thanks to the Peter Davies-owned pair Fontaine Collonges and Frero Banbou, who have both made it into this season's *Fifty*. Fontaine Collonges was sent off favourite for her race, a valuable mares' novice handicap chase and she showed a fair bit of improvement, looking to relish the conditions which weren't quite as testing as the official 'heavy' but softer than for her previous starts over fences. Fontaine Collonges stayed on strongly from two out and was well on top at the finish, 10 lengths clear of runner-up Wouldubewell.

That proved to be the last of Fontaine Collonges' four runs over fences, though she was taken out of a race at Cheltenham in April on account of the ground. She had made a very promising chasing debut at Wetherby in October over an inadequate trip and duly confirmed that when stepped up to two and a half miles for a mares' novice handicap at Warwick. Up with the pace throughout, she rallied to regain the lead at the final fence and stayed on well to beat Precious Eleanor by two and three quarter lengths. She finished behind that rival when fourth to the useful Vienna Court in a similar event at Cheltenham next time, but a bad mistake at the water didn't help her cause and she shaped as though crying out for either softer ground at the trip or a step up to three miles.

Longer distances should definitely suit Fontaine Collonges looking at her pedigree as she's by Bristol de Mai's sire Saddler Maker and, as her name suggests, related to the 2012 Grand National winner Neptune Collonges, who was a full brother to her dam. Fontaine Collonges is lightly raced all round—she won two of her four starts in bumpers, the first of those when trained in France, and had only three runs over hurdles, winning the third of them on heavy ground —so there should be more to come from her over fences. *Venetia Williams*

Conclusion: *Won two of her four starts in her first season over fences and has the potential to do better still when stepping up to 3m*

Frero Banbou (Fr)   c144
7 b.g. Apsis – Lady Banbou (Fr) (Useful (Fr))
2021/22 c16.8s^4 c16.4d^3 c16.3g^3 c16s* c15.5d^2 c15.9v^3 c15.8d Apr 7

Venetia Williams enjoyed her best seasonal total since 2013/14 last term, winning 60 races and a record prize money total which put her fifth in the trainers' championship. Leading novice chaser L'Homme Presse was one of two Cheltenham Festival winners, along with the Fulke Walwyn Kim Muir winner Chambard, while other highlights were provided by Cloudy Glen in the Ladbrokes Trophy, Royale Pagaille in the Peter Marsh Chase (for the second year in a row) and Funambule Sivola in the Game Spirit Chase.

Useful handicap chaser Frero Banbou had a good season, too, running each month from October through to April and finishing in the money in all bar his final start in the Red Rum Chase at Aintree when clearly not himself and probably ready for a break. That came just three weeks after one of his best efforts all season when finishing third to Global Citizen and Andy Dufresne in the Grand Annual at Cheltenham, though that was rather an odd performance from Frero Banbou, who was so detached at one point that he looked more likely to be pulled up than reach the frame before making good headway on the run to three out.

Frero Banbou had run below form on his reappearance at Ascot but fared better on his next couple of starts at Newbury and Cheltenham when third behind Il Ridoto—another member of this season's *Fifty*—and Editeur du Gite respectively. Frero Banbou had been ridden prominently up until that point, but regular partner Charlie Deutsch employed much more patient tactics for his next start at Lingfield's Winter Million meeting in January. That approach paid off as Frero Banbou, who'd not been that fluent early in the race, was produced to lead in the final 50 yards for a length win over Éclair d'Ainay, with the first two pulling a long way clear in testing conditions. On his only other start before Cheltenham, Frero Banbou ran well in defeat when again coming from well off the pace to pass the post only four lengths behind the well-handicapped winner Dolos.

The sturdy Frero Banbou, who acts on heavy ground, has raced only at around two miles but might be worth a try at a bit further. He's had two full seasons over fences, but he's still only seven and there should be more handicaps to be won with him. *Venetia Williams*

Conclusion: *Useful two-mile chaser who showed improved form in 2021/22 and can be forgiven his final start which was probably one run too many after a big effort at Cheltenham*

Gelino Bello (Fr)   h143p

6 b.g. Saint des Saints (Fr) – Parade (Fr) (Robin des Champs (Fr))
2021/22 h20g* h21d² h24g² h21v⁴ h20.5s* h24.7g* Apr 8

Two questions were raised when Gelino Bello ended last season with victory in the Grade 1 Sefton Novices' Hurdle at Aintree. Firstly, how high could Gelino Bello climb as a novice chaser this term? And secondly, just how good is Blazing Khal, the horse who defeated Gelino Bello in a pair of graded novice events at Cheltenham in the autumn but missed the rest of the campaign due to injury?

Hopefully, both questions will be answered this season as Blazing Khal is reportedly back in training with Charles Byrnes and Gelino Bello is all set to embark on a career over fences. That pair first met in the Grade 2 Ballymore Novices' Hurdle at Cheltenham's November Meeting for which neither of them started favourite, with that honour instead belonging to the Gordon Elliott-trained Off Your Rocco. Gelino Bello was sent off the 2/1 second favourite having created an excellent impression in three previous appearances, showing useful form in two starts in bumpers during the 2020/21 season and then making the perfect start to his hurdling career with a six-length victory in a maiden at Aintree last October.

Gelino Bello (left) should take high rank as a staying novice chaser

Gelino Bello built on the promise of that effort on his next outing at Cheltenham, but Blazing Khal was simply too good on the day and won by two and a half lengths. It was a similar a story when they met again in the Grade 2 Albert Bartlett Novices' Hurdle back at Cheltenham the following month, where Blazing Khal won by even further despite meeting Gelino Bello on 5 lb worse terms, ultimately landing the spoils by four and a quarter lengths.

That was Gelino Bello's first try over three miles and it was that trip which seemed to eke out a bit more improvement when he won the Sefton. In between, he finished fourth on his handicap debut in the Lanzarote Hurdle at Kempton and won an ordinary novice hurdle at Newbury for which he was sent off the 100/30-on favourite, both races run at around two and a half miles. Back up in trip at Aintree, Gelino Bello proved better than ever to gain his biggest success yet, asserting on the run-in after leading three out to win by four and a half lengths.

Santini, Champ and Ahoy Senor were the last three winners of the Sefton before Gelino Bello, so he certainly has some big shoes to fill. It will be no surprise if he proves up to the task, though, a tall gelding who appeals as an obvious type to make the grade over fences this season, particularly as his stamina is drawn out further. ***Paul Nicholls***

Conclusion: *No match for Blazing Khal when first tried in graded company as a novice hurdler but improved when winning the Sefton and looks one of the better prospects for novice chases in Britain over 3m+*

Adam Houghton (Gelino Bello): *"Few sires have thrown up good-quality staying chasers with the regularity that Saint des Saints has in recent years, with Djakadam, Protektorat and Saint Calvados all featuring among his best progeny. Gelino Bello is already one step ahead of that trio as a Grade 1-winning hurdler, which augurs well for his future prospects given that everything about him suggests he too will come into his own over fences. He can take high rank as a staying novice chaser this season."*

Gericault Roque (Fr)   c141p

6 b.g. Montmartre (Fr) – Nijinska Delaroque (Fr) (Lute Antique (Fr))

2021/22 c19.4d³ c23.6d² c26s² c29.2s² c25g² Mar 15

Gericault Roque's connections must be wondering how he didn't win a race last term. He was placed in all five of his races and found only one too good in the last four of them whilst going up a stone in the weights over the course of the season. On the other hand, he amassed a total of more than £50,000 in place money for those efforts and retains his novice status over fences for another season which gives him other options besides handicaps.

The good-topped Gericault Roque had won twice over two miles over hurdles, but his first season over fences revealed him to be very much a stayer. He made an encouraging debut over fences when third at Wetherby in October over a shorter trip, but it was when stepped up to three miles or more that he began to show useful form. Gericault Roque went closest to winning on his next start in a novice handicap at Chepstow when putting in his best work at the finish to go down by half a length to Pats Fancy. Although still only a five-year-old himself, he ran into a progressive four-year-old on his next start when coming up against Saint Palais in the Mandarin Handicap Chase at Newbury, beaten a length and a quarter whilst finishing clear of the rest.

It was a further step up in trip next for the Classic Handicap Chase at Warwick for which Gericault Roque was sent off favourite. He ran well enough to suggest he stayed the marathon trip and shaped quite well to split the pair who dominated the race from an early stage, Éclair Surf, who beat him 13 lengths, and Chirico Vallis. On his final start of the season, Gericault Roque had to run from 5 lb out of the handicap in the Ultima Handicap Chase at the Cheltenham Festival where he was fitted with a tongue strap for the first time over fences.

The first five home in the Ultima were all in their first season over fences and Gericault Roque ran his best race yet, fending off the eventual third Oscar Elite on the run-in but having no answer to Corach Rambler, who charged between them both to run out the winner by two and three-quarter lengths. Gericault Roque stuck to his task, though, and there is surely a top staying handicap with his name on it this season. **David Pipe**

Conclusion: *Progressed throughout his first season over fences when he kept finding one too good and well up to winning a good handicap this term with further improvement to come*

Get A Tonic (Ire) h131
6 b.m. Getaway (Ger) – Atomic Winner (Ire) (Poliglote)
2021/22 h15.8s² h20.5g* h19.9v* h20.3s³ h21d² h24.4v² h24.3d* Apr 1

There are plenty of Dan Skelton-trained horses in this year's *Fifty*, all of which points to another productive season for the handler. It will certainly be a surprise if he can't place Get A Tonic to advantage in the months ahead, a smart mare who is likely to be in search of more black type.

Get A Tonic had a busy campaign last term, making a total of seven starts over hurdles. After filling the runner-up spot on her debut in that sphere in a mares' maiden at Uttoxeter in October, she then showed much improved form to win her next two starts, easily getting off the mark in a similar event at Leicester in November and then beating the boys to follow up in a novice hurdle back at Uttoxeter three weeks later, always doing enough there to land the spoils by three and a quarter lengths.

A step up in class beckoned after those wins and Get A Tonic's next three starts all came at listed level, first against geldings at Cheltenham on New Year's Day where she was beaten 13 lengths into third behind Hillcrest. She then followed that run with a career best back against her own sex at Warwick, when getting within three lengths of the subsequent dual Grade 1 winner Marie's Rock, and a first win at listed level probably would have been hers had things panned out differently at Doncaster next time. Stepped up to three miles for the first time, she really ought to have won on Town Moor, meeting trouble when first trying to improve and then veering on the run-in with the winner in her sights, ultimately being beaten half a length by Fonzerelli.

Compensation for that defeat came when Get A Tonic was last seen making her handicap debut at Ayr's Scottish Grand National meeting in April. She didn't need to improve there to capitalise on a good opening mark, essentially a cut above those who remained following the fall of her main rival, Aurora Thunder, at the final flight, keeping on well to beat Motown Maggie by a length and a half.

A strong-travelling sort, Get A Tonic clearly stays well but isn't short of pace either. She will have plenty of options in graded mares' events over trips ranging from two and a half miles to three miles, with all roads surely leading to the David Nicholson Mares' Hurdle at the Cheltenham Festival. She should be able to pick up a race or two along the way and could easily develop into one of the main British contenders for that Grade 1. **Dan Skelton**

Conclusion: *Useful-looking mare who achieved plenty in her first season over hurdles and should be capable of making an even bigger impact in graded company this term*

Godrevy Point (Fr) h117
6 b.g. Coastal Path – Quetzalya (Fr) (Assessor (Ire))
2021/22 b15.8d³ h20g⁵ h20.8d² h19.4d² h25.5s* h24.3m³ Mar 23

The 2021/22 National Hunt season was a highly successful one for trainer Richard Bandey based on pretty much whichever metric you use. The burgeoning stable sent out 19 winners, dwarfing the previous campaign's tally of two, and a strike rate of 24% was surpassed by only Willie Mullins (26.05%) among trainers who had at least 50 runners. Bandey was also prominent when sorting by Timeform's run-to-form percentage—he was behind only Gary Hanmer among British-based trainers—while backing each of his runners would have resulted in a healthy level-stake profit of £23.02.

Bandey, whose exploits last season are profiled in greater depth in our Rising Star section, has also made a good start to the current campaign from the handful of runners he has sent out and one who we think it will pay to follow is Godrevy Point.

Godrevy Point's five outings over hurdles last season yielded only one win, which came when sent off the 9/2-on favourite in a weak maiden at Hereford in February, but he has all the ingredients to develop into a better chaser this term. He is a tall, unfurnished six-year-old with the scope to take well to chasing, while the accuracy with which he jumped when chasing home fellow *Fifty* member Skytastic in a maiden hurdle at Doncaster in January also augurs well for his prospects over fences.

Godrevy Point failed to build on that form in two subsequent starts, making heavy weather of landing the odds at Hereford before failing to justify favouritism on his handicap debut at Haydock, but the subsequent break should have done him good and allowed him to fill his frame. Bandey impressed with how he placed his horses last season, racking up sequences with the likes of Saint Palais and Give Me A Moment, and he should have plenty of suitable handicap options with Godrevy Point, who is effective over trips ranging from two and a half miles to three and a quarter miles. *Richard Bandey*

Conclusion: *Chasing type on looks who can leave his hurdles efforts behind over fences for an upwardly mobile yard*

Harbour Lake (Ire)   h134p

6 br.g. Shantou (USA) – Aibrean (Ire) (Winged Love (Ire))
2021/22 h16d* h16v* h19.6s^bd h19.6v* Mar 13

Harbour Lake is the second of three horses in this year's *Fifty* who sport the colours of the late Trevor Hemmings. East Street was the first of them—included with a view to his future in staying chases—and Harbour Lake is essentially cut from the same cloth. However, rather than embarking on a novice chasing campaign straight away, it will be no surprise if Harbour Lake is kept over hurdles this season, looking very much the type to win more handicaps in that sphere.

A son of Shantou from the family of a smart staying chaser in Fine Rightly, Harbour Lake was backed at long odds when making his debut in a two-mile novice hurdle at Wetherby last October. In the event, that confidence proved fully justified as he looked something out of the ordinary in making a winning start to his career, finishing with a rare flourish to land the spoils by four and a half lengths. Back over the same course and distance in December, he was sent off the 13/8-on favourite this time and duly shrugged off a penalty to make it two from two, once again impressing with his strength at the finish as he forged 11 lengths clear.

Harbour Lake's sights were raised next time as he headed to Huntingdon for the listed Sidney Banks Memorial Novices' Hurdle. However, his inexperience shone through in those deeper waters as he made a series of novicey mistakes, already looking held in a share of fourth when brought down at the last.

But while Harbour Lake may have lost his unbeaten record at Huntingdon, his potential remained intact and he got firmly back on track when last seen making a successful handicap debut at Bangor in March. That was his second start over two and a half miles and he faced another member of the *Fifty* in the shape of Jungle Jack. From an opening BHA mark of 126, Harbour Lane ultimately proved three and three-quarter lengths too good for that rival after both made a mistake at the last, just needing to be kept up to his work from there to assert.

Harbour Lake is still unexposed, both in general and with a view to stepping up further in trip. He will certainly stay beyond two and a half miles—in keeping with the stamina in his pedigree—and a BHA mark of 130 remains a good starting point to this season when good-quality handicap hurdles are likely to be on his agenda. **Alan King**

Conclusion: *Won all three of his completed starts over hurdles and looks the type to progress through the ranks in handicaps as his stamina is drawn out further*

Il Ridoto (Fr) c139
5 b.g. Kapgarde (Fr) – L'Exploratrice (Fr) (Trempolino (USA))
2021/22 c16.3d³ c16.4d* c15.5dᵖᵘ c16s³ c15.9v c20.5g³ Apr 2

Paul Nicholls isn't averse to putting a four-year-old over fences if he feels he's got the right type of horse, often a French import with some chasing experience already. Frodon was a notable example, winning the Caspian Caviar Gold Cup at Cheltenham at that age in 2016. It certainly didn't do him any harm, as he has won another 10 chases since his novice season, including a Ryanair Chase, a King George VI Chase and, last season, the Champion Chase at Down Royal.

Il Ridoto might not turn out to be another Frodon, but he has made a promising start to his chasing career at the same age. He too had already run over fences in France, finishing second on his completed start, having earlier won twice over hurdles at Pau for Hector de Lageneste and Guillaume Macaire. Il Ridoto faded out of contention on his debut for Nicholls at Newton Abbot in October but was a completely different proposition on his next start at Newbury on Ladbrokes Trophy day. Taking on a competitive field of more experienced handicappers, Il Ridoto travelled strongly in mid-division before leading two out and quickening clear on the flat to win with plenty in hand by six and a half lengths from Numitor.

Il Ridoto failed to add to that win but had some valid excuses afterwards and remains one to be positive about. He was pulled up when turned out quickly for the Henry VIII Novices' Chase at Sandown just a week after Newbury and then didn't see his races out in testing conditions on his next two starts in a novice at Lingfield (won by the Henry VIII runner-up War Lord, who'd also beaten him at Newton Abbott) and back in handicap company in the Grand Annual at the Cheltenham Festival when shaping much better than a well-held eighth would suggest.

Back on a sound surface, Il Ridoto signed off for the season with a creditable third behind Do Your Job and Minella Drama in the Future Champions Novices' Chase at Ayr on his first attempt at two and a half miles, only losing second close home. He shares his sire Kapgarde with stablemate Clan des Obeaux and the latest Gold Cup winner A Plus Tard, so there is stamina in the pedigree and he might see out two and a half miles more thoroughly given another summer to strengthen. **Paul Nicholls**

Conclusion: *Won a competitive handicap at Newbury in good style and, still a lightly-raced five-year-old, looks well up to winning more races over fences*

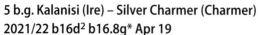

Imperial Merlin (Ire)   b101

5 b.g. Kalanisi (Ire) – Silver Charmer (Charmer)
2021/22 b16d² b16.8g* Apr 19

John Quinn enjoyed plenty of success over the summer with the high-class sprinter Highfield Princess, but the yard's jumpers always command respect, too, and Imperial Merlin looks one to follow through the winter months. He made his debut at Wetherby the week after the Cheltenham Festival in a bumper that has been won in recent seasons by horses who have gone on to better things over jumps, including Kalashnikov and Hillcrest. The latest edition was contested by runners from the stables of Paul Nicholls, Dan Skelton, Fergal O'Brien and Olly Murphy, and it was one of Murphy's newcomers, Chasing Fire, an expensive purchase from the pointing field, who showed the most speed having been heavily backed beforehand.

Imperial Merlin shaped promisingly two lengths back in second, making good progress in the back straight and then showing his inexperience when running green and hanging left before staying on to pull three and a half lengths clear of the Skelton newcomer Hitching Jacking in third. The overall impression was that it was a good-quality bumper, though the form hasn't really been tested as Imperial Merlin is the only one to have run since. He was found a considerably weaker bumper at Sedgefield the following month facing a couple of newcomers and one who'd been beaten out of sight on his debut. Imperial Merlin started long odds on and won every bit as decisively as the betting suggested, going on approaching the home turn and quickening clear in the straight for a ready nine-length win from Tommy's Fortune.

Bought for €34,000 as a three-year-old, Imperial Merlin has a good jumping pedigree. His sire Kalanisi has produced the likes of Champion Hurdle winner Katchit, the aforementioned Kalashnikov and another high-class chaser, Imperial Aura, who is in the same ownership as Imperial Merlin. His dam Silver Charmer was a dual winner of the listed mares' handicap hurdle at Cheltenham's April meeting and has already produced a high-class chaser in Secret Investor, winner of the Denman Chase in 2021 for Paul Nicholls. Imperial Merlin is therefore bred to stay further than two miles when he goes over hurdles and he looks sure to do well in novice contests. *John Quinn*

Conclusion: *Ran into an above-average type on his bumper debut before landing the odds in a weaker race next time and looks a good prospect for novice hurdles in the North*

Jonbon (Fr)   h153p

6 b.g. Walk In The Park (Ire) – Star Face (Fr) (Saint des Saints (Fr))
2021/22 h16.3d* h15.7d* h15.7s* h16.4g² h16.5g* Apr 8

Jonbon has always carried the burden of a big reputation with him and with good reason. He's a full brother to an outstanding jumper in Douvan and he fetched a record-breaking £570,000 when bought by J. P. McManus after winning his only start in Irish points, while

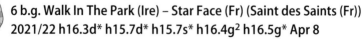

a successful Rules debut in a Newbury bumper in the spring of 2021 did nothing to lessen expectations ahead of Jonbon's jumping career.

But if Jonbon began last season as his stable's most exciting hurdling prospect, the main weight of expectations quickly shifted to stablemate Constitution Hill after the unbeaten pair had clashed in the Supreme Novices' Hurdle at the Cheltenham Festival. Jonbon ran well, leading three out after travelling well close to the pace, but he was left behind when Constitution Hill took over soon after jumping the second last and quickened away to win by 22 lengths in the manner of an exceptional novice.

That defeat takes some of the heat off Jonbon, but he remains no less an exciting prospect in his own right, particularly as he'll be starting a new chapter in his career over fences this season while Constitution Hill remains over hurdles. After Cheltenham, Jonbon ended the season with a Grade 1 win of his own in the Top Novices' Hurdle at Aintree, a race Darlan, My Tent Or Yours and Buveur d'Air had all won for the same connections after being placed in the Supreme. Jonbon was made to fight for his win, having only a neck to spare over the Willie Mullins-trained runner-up El Fabiolo with the pair a long way clear of the rest, but the gritty nature of that success reflected well on him given that he hadn't been hard pressed to win his three races prior to Cheltenham, none of which were truly-run affairs.

Jonbon jumps the last on his way to victory at Ascot

Jonbon began with an impressive victory in a maiden at Newbury in November before Grade 2 successes in the Kennel Gate Novices' Hurdle at Ascot and the Rossington Main Novices' Hurdle at Haydock. Jonbon won well again at Ascot whereas at Haydock, where he was conceding 5 lb all round and came home three lengths clear of Richmond Lake, the way the race developed wasn't conducive to such an impressive display. Jonbon is a big, well-made gelding, just the type to take to fences. He may not have emulated Douvan in the Supreme, but it could be a different story in the Arkle. **Nicky Henderson**

Conclusion: *No disgrace in his only defeat to date at the hands of top-notch stablemate Constitution Hill and looks a worthy favourite to become his stable's eighth Arkle winner*

Jungle Jack h131

6 ch.g. Doyen (Ire) – Skew (Niniski (USA))
2021/22 h16.8s* h15.7v* h16.7s* h19.6v² Mar 13

Having been fortunate enough to enjoy many golden moments with former stars Overturn and Peddlers Cross, trainer Donald McCain and owner Tim Leslie clearly know a horse with a fine attitude when they see one and they have another tough type on their hands in Jungle Jack..

Jungle Jack won his sole start between the flags in October 2020 but wasn't seen in public for well over a year after that. It was worth the wait when he did eventually make his debut under Rules for his new connections, though, justifying strong market support to win a maiden hurdle at Sedgefield in December. The last of his six leaps (they omitted the penultimate flight) was arguably his best and, despite seemingly getting a little tired—or perhaps just a fraction lonely—on the run-in, he never looked in any serious danger of coming unstuck, ultimately landing the spoils by a length.

There was more to come, too, as Jungle Jack went on to complete a hat-trick in novice company. He showed a good attitude to defy a penalty at Haydock later in December, knuckling down well to win by half a length, before then taking another step forward to make it three from three at Bangor in February, overcoming a double penalty this time and doing it comfortably by 11 lengths.

Jungle Jack ended last season with a creditable second on his handicap debut back at Bangor in March, losing his unbeaten record but confirming himself a useful novice. That race was run over two and a half miles and he clearly stayed the longer trip well having raced exclusively at around two miles prior to that, passing the post less than four lengths behind fellow *Fifty* member Harbour Lake and leaving the impression it would have been closer still had he negotiated the last better.

A straightforward ride, Jungle Jack is the type to go on improving as his stamina is drawn out further and a BHA mark of 125 is highly unlikely to prove his limit. His connections are considering starting this season over hurdles, but everything about him suggests he'll really come into his own over fences. Not only is he a winning pointer, but he is also a brother to the useful hurdler/high-class chaser Valdez and a half-brother to the fair hurdler/fairly useful chaser Skewiff, both of whom were much better over fences than they were over hurdles. **Donald McCain**

Conclusion: *Beaten just once in four starts over hurdles and remains with handicapping scope from a BHA mark of 125; very much the type to make a chaser when the time comes, too*

Kateira

b100

5 b.m. Kayf Tara – Raitera (Fr) (Astarabad (USA))
2021/22 b15.8s* b17d⁵ Apr 7

A half-sister to three winners, Kateira had something to live up to before she even made it to the racecourse, but it didn't take her long to provide dam Raitera—who is herself a half-sister to the top-class chaser Golden Silver—with a fourth individual winner.

Sent to Huntingdon in February for her bumper debut, Kateira faced a rival in Kalelula who had racecourse experience to call upon having made a promising start to her career at Wetherby the previous month, staying on well to be beaten just a length and a half. However, she was put in her place much more comprehensively at Huntingdon by Kateira, who was simply in a different league. Dropped out in the early stages, she made steady headway out wide and was produced to lead a furlong out before storming clear to beat the market leader by five and a half lengths.

Kateira looked well worth a try at a higher level, such was the impression she created at Huntingdon, and she got her opportunity in the Grade 2 mares' bumper on the opening day of the Grand National meeting. One of the leading British-trained contenders at 7/1, she was arguably a bit disappointing there on face value, passing the post 16 lengths behind the winner in fifth. There were mitigating circumstances, however, as she was the only one from the back to make any sort of headway in a steadily-run race, staying on well but never threatening to get on terms with the principals.

Kateira is essentially better judged on her debut effort which suggests she is a useful prospect for novice hurdling against her own sex this season. There is certainly a strong programme for her to exploit in that division and she could be the type to run up a sequence before testing the waters again in better company. **Dan Skelton**

Conclusion: *Showed lots of ability on debut and had valid excuses when failing to repeat that effort next time; should be capable of winning novice hurdles against her own sex*

Follow us on Twitter @Timeform

Knickerbockerglory (Ire) h124

6 b.g. Fame And Glory – The Brass Lady (Ire) (Supreme Leader)
2021/22 h16d⁴ h15.7g⁵ h16.5s* h15.2d³ h15.8v* h16.2d* Apr 22

Named after a dessert craved by children across the globe for its ice cream content and distinctive long spoon required to eat it, here's another horse we're sweet on from the Dan Skelton yard this season.

Successful on the second of his two starts in bumpers when trained by Alastair Ralph, it's fair to say that Knickerbockerglory made an inauspicious debut for Skelton in a novice hurdle at Wetherby in October. Skelton had won the two previous runnings with Proschema and Third Time Lucki and Knickerbockerglory was sent off the 5/4 favourite to complete the hat-trick, but he was back to racing very freely, just as he had on his bumper debut. Having pulled so hard, his challenge petered out going to the last and he eventually passed the post around nine and a half lengths behind the winner in fourth.

From there Knickerbockerglory went to Haydock for a listed novice hurdle on Betfair Chase day where Harry Skelton was at pains to get the horse to relax. Steadied at the start and dropped right out in a tactical race, he made smooth headway three out but could never muster a challenge. Still, the Timeform report predicted that he was "sure to improve and win races over hurdles"—and so it proved as he ended the campaign with three wins from four starts, his only defeat in that sequence coming when third on his handicap debut at Wincanton.

The key was to let Knickerbockerglory bowl along in front. The new tactics were first employed in a maiden hurdle at Taunton in January where he impressed with how he travelled and jumped, steadily drawing clear from three out to win unchallenged by 15 lengths. After his reversal at Wincanton later that month, he then justified very short odds in novice hurdles at Ludlow in March and Perth in April, beating inferior rivals by an aggregate margin of around 25 lengths.

It remains to be seen whether Knickerbockerglory will stay over hurdles or embark on a chasing career this season, but he remains very much one to keep on the right side either way. He isn't especially scopey but has the demeanour and athleticism to prove at least as good over fences, particularly as his style of racing is likely to take plenty out of their comfort zone. He could be an exhilarating sight and the sort to run up a sequence as he gains in experience. *Dan Skelton*

Conclusion: *Won three novice hurdles when allowed to dominate and possesses so much speed that he could be a real force in novice chases at around 2m*

La Cavsa Nostra (Ire)   c122

10 b.g. Flemensfirth (USA) – Pharenna (Ire) (Phardante (Fr))
2021/22 c26.2s^{pu} c25.2d* Feb 27

The fairly useful chaser La Cavsa Nostra appeals as one of the more interesting contenders in the veteran ranks this season, particularly given the record of Wiltshire trainer Neil Mulholland, who has proved himself very adept with similar types in the last few years. For example, Carole's Destrier, Fr Humphrey and Soupy Soups have all won veterans' chases since 2019, while La Cavsa Nostra himself is already off the mark in such company.

A winning pointer, La Cavsa Nostra offered little in his first three starts for Mulholland during the 2018/19 season, finishing down the field in a couple of maiden hurdles before meeting with the same fate when set a stiff task on his chasing debut. However, given an eight-month break between his first two runs over fences, he then left that effort well behind when switched to a handicap at Chepstow in October 2019, running out a resounding six-length winner from Christmas In April.

Possible fragility might be why La Cavsa Nostra has made only four starts since then and, after registering a second success over fences at Sedgefield in November 2019, he then spent 27 months on the sidelines before being pulled up on his belated reappearance back at Chepstow in February this year. There were other excuses for that below-par effort, though, never going well after being badly hampered at the fifth, and he showed that he still retains all his ability when following that effort with a determined victory in a veterans' event at Hereford later in the month, staying on well to land the spoils by a length and a quarter.

That Hereford victory was his first run against fellow veterans and his third win from just six starts over fences overall. That makes him attractively lightly raced if he goes down the veterans' route again this season, with all roads surely leading to the Series Final at Sandown in January. **Neil Mulholland**

Conclusion: *Hasn't got many miles on the clock for a veteran and his Hereford success when last seen identified him as one for the shortlist in similar events this season*

Lac de Constance (Fr)   h127p

6 gr.g. Martaline – Kendova (Fr) (Kendor (Fr))
2021/22 h16.7s* h16.7v* h16s* Mar 13

After being bought for €135,000 as a three-year-old, Lac de Constance has so far been a work in progress for his top team and remains a fascinating prospect. From a very good French jumping family—his dam is a half-sister to the high-class hurdler Paul's Saga—he was restricted to two runs in bumpers, finishing third at Warwick in December 2020 and again hinting there was more to come when fifth at Uttoxeter the following March.

The first sighting of Lac de Constance last season came in a maiden hurdle at Exeter in December where he made a stylish debut over obstacles, a breathing operation during his break evidently having done him some good. Patiently ridden having been bumped at the first, he made a mistake at the next flight but soon recovered and, having been upsides the leaders two out, came clear with plenty in hand to beat Great Ocean by eight and a half lengths.

Lac de Constance returned to Exeter nine weeks later for a listed novice hurdle and, despite still showing signs of inexperience after hitting the front, his unbeaten record over timber never looked in danger. Tracking the pace to the second last, Harry Skelton sent him to the front soon after. His mount had the race in safe keeping from there but did hang right on the run-in and had to be kept up to his work to beat Peking Rose by two and three-quarter lengths.

There was no temptation to head to one of the big spring festivals and instead Lac de Constance was sent to Warwick under a double penalty on the Sunday before Cheltenham. Sent off the 11/2-on favourite, he made the most of a simple opportunity to complete the hat-trick, simply proving a class above his rivals. He came clear from two out and, having been briefly put under pressure after the last, smoothly swept 12 lengths clear of Ben Bulben.

Lac de Constance has been kept fairly low-key so far—his listed victory notwithstanding—but he looks capable of making his presence felt at a higher level, with chasing an exciting proposition for this season. He is very much the type to progress through the ranks in that sphere and will stay at least two and a half miles having been campaigned exclusively at around two miles over hurdles. **Dan Skelton**

Conclusion: *Remains with untapped potential after going unbeaten in his novice season over hurdles and looks a smart prospect for novice chasing this term; will stay 2½m+*

Leave of Absence (Fr)   b111+
5 ch.g. Masked Marvel – To Much Fun (Act One)
2021/22 b16d* b16.3g* b17d³ Apr 9

Chris Gordon has trained a couple of high-quality novice hurdlers in recent years, namely Highway One O Two and Aucunrisque—another member of this year's *Fifty*—both of whom graduated from bumpers. Aucunrisque ran in points before he contested bumpers and Leave of Absence has been treading a similar path having had his first taste of competitive action when third in an Irish point in November last year.

That good showing ensured Leave of Absence was sent off a well-backed 9/2 chance on his debut for Gordon in a Kempton bumper just under three months later, the positive market move reflecting stable confidence which was justified as he ran out an impressive seven-length winner. He then spent seven weeks on the sidelines before making the most of a good opportunity to follow up at Newbury in April, taking his time to assert but doing so very well by the end to beat Nicky Henderson's Boom Boom, who had also been behind him at Kempton, by six lengths.

There was no time for Leave of Absence to rest on his laurels and he reappeared just seven days later in the Grade 2 bumper at Aintree, a race won by the likes of The New One, Barters Hill, Lalor and McFabulous in the last decade alone. Incidentally, the list of beaten horses in that contest in the same timeframe is arguably just as impressive, with My Tent Or Yours, Bellshill, Buveur d'Air, Ballyandy, Willoughby Court, If The Cap Fits, Al Dancer and Stage Star all coming up short there before going on to achieve a high level over jumps.

A third place for Leave of Absence should be viewed as a major positive then, again just taking time to hit full stride as the race took shape. Beaten only three and a quarter lengths behind Lookaway, he kept on well in the manner of one set to stay further than two miles over hurdles and it will be a big surprise if he isn't capable of winning races as a novice this season. **Chris Gordon**

Conclusion: *Showed useful form in just three starts in bumpers and looks capable of scaling similar heights as a novice hurdler this season; will stay further than 2m*

Ben Linfoot (Leave of Absence): *"The signs are Masked Marvel is going to turn into a good National Hunt stallion, Teahupoo's exploits the earliest hint we have of that, and his son Leave of Absence looks a novice hurdler to follow for the excellent Chris Gordon. Beaten horses who fared well in the Grade 2 Aintree bumper have shone in recent seasons (think My Tent Of Yours and Buveur d'Air) and this five-year-old looks likely to make his mark in novice hurdles, just like stablemates Highway One O Two and Aucunrisque have the last couple of campaigns."*

Luke   h115p
5 b.g. Lucarno (USA) – More Ballet Money (Old Vic)
2021/22 h16.2d³ h19.4v³ h20.6d² h20.1d* Mar 17

Mick and David Easterby have been very patient with Luke and there looks to be plenty more to come from the five-year-old this season. He was restricted to just one outing in 2020/2021, making his debut in a Hexham bumper in the spring. He shaped throughout as if needing the experience—or at least that was the hope given his family isn't without temperament—doing his best work at the finish despite carrying his head a bit awkwardly.

Luke returned to Hexham for his hurdling debut in a two-mile novice in November where he again offered something to work on, finding himself short of room on the home turn but keeping on well for third in the manner of one likely to have more to offer as he stepped up in trip. Admittedly, it didn't happen immediately when he ran over two and a half miles at Doncaster in December, simply matching his debut form there in a well-beaten third, but he went much closer at Market Rasen next time where he probably should have won, conceding first run to Hometown Hero before staying on strongly to get within a neck of that rival at the line.

The temptation must have been there to switch to handicaps, but instead Luke was found a good opportunity to get off the mark in a maiden hurdle run over two and a half miles back at Hexham in March. Sent off the 13/8-on favourite, he probably didn't need to improve to gain his first success, but there was plenty to like about the way he responded to run down his main market rival, rallying well after the last to get the verdict by a nose.

The rangy Luke still has longer trips to explore (yet to race beyond 21 furlongs) and remains open to improvement with that in mind, particularly when he makes the switch to handicaps. A BHA mark of 116 looks a fair starting point to life in that sphere and his physique suggests he is the type to take well to chasing when the time comes, too.
Michael & David Easterby

Conclusion: *Type to make a chaser but possibly has unfinished business over hurdles in the short term, still looking very much a work a progress in four starts last season; will stay further than 21f and one to be interested in with a view to staying handicaps*

Dan Barber (Luke): *"Sometimes a horse just sticks in the mind even after a mere fleeting glance in a paddock on travels around various racecourses. Luke was one of those, standing out a mile in the parade ring at Market Rasen, and everything about him suggests he's going to make a very useful novice over fences; he's a strapping sort from a family featuring no shortage of chase winners."*

Magic Wave   b97
6 b.g. Gentlewave (Ire) – Annie's Gift (Ire) (Presenting)
2021/22 b16.6v² b16g² Apr 2

It's fair to say that Mark Walford wouldn't be renowned for his runners in bumpers. After all, he had career figures of two winners from 45 runners in such races up to the end of the 2021/22 National Hunt season and even Magic Wave, the best bumper horse he has trained on Timeform ratings, failed to get off the mark in two attempts last term.

It's worth focusing on the positives, though, and Magic Wave certainly showed enough in those two starts to suggest he'll be winning races somewhere down the line, filling the runner-up spot both times and achieving a fairly useful level of form in the process.

Backed at long odds before his debut at Doncaster in March, Magic Wave was held up in the early stages before starting to make headway inside the final four furlongs. He showed signs of greenness (hung left under pressure) but still picked off every rival bar the favourite Spring Meadow, who had the benefit of a previous run at Ffos Las the previous month. Beaten just two and a half lengths at the line, Magic Wave then produced an even better effort when finding only Autumn Return too strong at Ayr's

Scottish Grand National fixture, not going down without a fight against a rival with the experience of three point runs to call upon, rallying well to be beaten just a head.

Ironically, Autumn Return is trained by Ruth Jefferson and that yard has had bags of success with some of Magic Wave's immediate family over the years. They include the bumper winner/fairly useful hurdler Black Ivory, a half-brother to Magic Wave, and the useful hurdler/smart chaser According To Pete, a half-brother to Magic Wave's unraced dam.

It's certainly a good jumping family and the one thing that they mostly have in common is that they stay well. Magic Wave really ought to flourish over jumps and his progress over hurdles this season is eagerly anticipated, particularly when he goes up in trip and switches to handicaps further down the line. **Mark Walford**

Conclusion: *Bred to stay well and shaped in kind in two starts in bumpers; looks the sort to make big strides when tackling 2½m+ over hurdles*

Make My Day (Ire)   h110p
6 b.g. Galileo (Ire) – Posset (Oasis Dream)
2021/22 h16.3d h19.2s² h17.7g³:: 2022 F16g² F16g² F20m F20.4m F16m Aug 6

Steven Packham's red and white silks have most famously been carried to success by Goshen, a two-time Grade 2 winner who is probably better known for the most dramatic of unseats when clear at the last in the 2020 JCB Triumph Hurdle at the Cheltenham Festival. Bar the Champion Chase winner Sire de Grugy, a terrific horse who won five times at Grade 1 level in total, Goshen would be one of the best horses Gary Moore has trained and there is no doubt that he gets a higher-class of horse into his West Sussex yard these days.

Make My Day isn't likely to be a Goshen or a Sire de Grugy, but he's got a familiar profile to many a handicap project from his stable from over the years, well-established as useful on the Flat but still only scratching the surface of what he can do over hurdles.

Make My Day has had 11 starts on the level and has proved himself a worthy 90+ rated horse this summer, finishing a close-up second off marks in the low-90s at Ascot in May and Goodwood in June. He was subsequently below form when running over two and a half miles at both Royal Ascot and Glorious Goodwood, leaving the firm impression he's not an out-and-out stayer on the Flat. He then ran better but didn't appear to have any obvious excuses when dropped back to two miles at the Shergar Cup at Ascot, so his connections will surely be turning their attentions to handicap hurdles this winter in search of more winnable opportunities.

Make My Day was given a BHA mark of 104 after running three times over hurdles within the space of four weeks in February/March and that looks lenient judged by the level he's been running to on the Flat. He's very much one to keep on the right side. **Gary Moore**

Conclusion: *Showed just fair form in three qualifying runs over hurdles but should be able to leave those efforts behind in handicaps if his useful Flat form is any guide*

Ned Tanner (Ire)   h113

6 b.g. Milan – Rose Tanner (Ire) (Roselier (Fr))

2021/22 b16v⁴ h20s⁴ h24.3s³ h22.7v* h24.3v³ h19.5s* Mar 12

This season Nick Alexander and his team must face up to life without stable stalwart Lake View Lad, who was retired in March this year after showing signs that he was on the downgrade at the age of 12. A very smart chaser at his best, Lake View Lad made his debut for Alexander back in November 2015 and bowed out with a record of nine wins from 33 starts under Rules, notably giving the yard its biggest success yet when winning the 2020 Many Clouds Chase at Aintree.

Horses capable of competing at that level are obviously very hard to come by, but Alexander can look to the future with plenty of optimism after he enjoyed the best season of his training career to date in 2021/22, saddling 35 winners and earning over £335,000 in total prize money. The highlight came at Ayr in March when the trainer brought up a 2,193/1 five-timer at Ayr.

One of those winners was Ned Tanner, who appeals as one of the more interesting youngsters coming through the ranks at Kinneston. Ned Tanner improved throughout his novice season over hurdles, getting off the mark at the third attempt at Kelso in December where he just needed to be driven out to land the spoils by a length and three-quarters. He then made his handicap debut over three miles at Ayr in February and shaped a bit better than the bare result in third, passing the post less than four lengths behind the winner despite leaving the impression he would have benefited from a stronger gallop.

Ned Tanner was last seen on that famous March afternoon for Alexander. He was well backed down in trip to two and a half miles and looked value for extra as he gained his first success in handicaps, impressing with the way he went through the race and probably idling after being produced to lead soon after three out. He always doing enough to hold on from there, ultimately winning by a length and a half.

Ned Tanner still looks one step ahead of the handicapper from a BHA mark of 117 and a switch to chasing this season promises to unlock further progress. He should be up to winning more handicaps in that discipline, particularly in the depths of winter when the mud is flying (has raced solely on soft/heavy going so far). **N. W. Alexander**

Conclusion: *Likeable type who improved with racing over hurdles last season and should continue in a similar vein over fences*

Netywell (Fr) h119p

5 b.g. Willywell (Fr) – Netova (Fr) (Network (Ger))
2021/22 h16.2d⁴ h16s² h17s⁴ h16v* Mar 7

Kinross trainer Lucinda Russell saddled 46 winners in Britain last season, enjoying her most prolific campaign since 2017/18 when she equalled that tally, while she also earned over £750,000 in total prize money, her biggest haul since 2016/17 when One For Arthur pocketed over £560,000 for winning the Grand National alone.

Last season certainly wasn't short of highlights either as Corach Rambler won the Ultima Handicap Chase at the Cheltenham Festival and Ahoy Senor—another member of the *Fifty*—bounced back from his defeat at the Festival with a convincing victory in the Grade 1 Mildmay Novices' Chase at Aintree to mark himself out as a future Cheltenham Gold Cup contender.

As those two victories underline, steeplechasers are Russell's bread and butter and, in the shape of Netywell, she has an exciting novice to unleash this winter. By Willywell, a three-time listed winner on the Flat in France, and out of Netova, a winner both on the Flat and over hurdles in the same country, Netywell has an unfashionable pedigree, but he has shown promise ever since he appeared in a Kelso bumper in the spring of 2021.

Fourth there, Netywell repeated that finishing position on his hurdling debut at Perth five months later, where a late error halted his progress, and he improved on that again on his second start over hurdles when filling the runner-up spot in a maiden at Ayr in January. Another bad mistake at the last at Carlisle in February prevented him from building on that, but he put it all together on his final start at Wetherby in March, quickening clear in the straight having travelled smoothly to win by five and a half lengths.

Netywell was entitled to win that race on form, but it was nice to see him deliver on his promise with a confidence-boosting win and, still only a five-year-old, this lengthy gelding has the physique to thrive when he makes the switch to chasing this season.
Lucinda Russell

Conclusion: *Showed just fair form over hurdles but very much the type to blossom over fences given his size and one to keep on the right side in novice chases in the North*

Simon Walker (Netywell): *"Size mightn't be everything, but it sure helps when it comes to jumping fences and, if physique is anything to go by, it's hard to believe that Netywell won't develop into a smashing novice chaser. The fact he's got an opening BHA mark of just 111 is a bonus and, if he was mine, Netywell would be going straight over fences in an attempt to rattle up a sequence. If he's got the athleticism to match his size then he'll surely win plenty of races in 2022/23"*

North Lodge (Ire) h145

5 b.g. Presenting – Saddleeruppat (Ire) (Saddlers' Hall (Ire))
2021/22 h17v* h20.3d* h18.1s² h20d³ Apr 9

North Lodge looked the part on paper before his debut in a novice hurdle at Aintree in December and he didn't disappoint. A son of Presenting and a half-brother to the useful hurdler/smart chaser Winter Escape, from the family of the high-class hurdler Black Jack Ketchum, North Lodge was very professional on deep ground at the Merseyside track. Ridden to close on the leaders going to the last, he knuckled down well from there to beat a pair of previous winners, Bombs Away and Richmond Lake—another member of the *Fifty*—by a neck.

From there it was graded company all the way. North Lodge's next appearance was in the Grade 2 Ballymore Novices' Hurdle at Cheltenham on Festival Trials Day in January and, despite showing signs of greenness by hanging right after hitting the front, he ultimately proved two and a half lengths too good for Balco Coastal. That was over two and a half miles and he dropped back a couple of furlongs next time for the Grade 2 Premier Novices' Hurdle at Kelso. He met with defeat for the first time in Scotland but still emerged as the best horse at the weights, passing the post just a short head behind the more experienced Nells Son (who received 5 lb) having looked likely to prevail at one stage, with the first two pulling clear of the remainder.

North Lodge edges to the front at Cheltenham

The Timeform race report included the line "lost his unbeaten record—and with it, perhaps, any thoughts of him being a high-class novice", but a Grade 1 contest was next, namely the Mersey Novices' Hurdle back over two and a half miles at Aintree. While unable to improve on his previous efforts, North Lodge was by no means disgraced there as he finished a never-nearer third, beaten eight and a half lengths, behind Three Stripe Life and Might I.

Crucially, North Lodge again left the impression at Aintree that he may yet have more to offer when faced with a greater emphasis on stamina. A step up to three miles is certainly worth trying and he starts the new campaign on a BHA mark of 142. That appeals as being potentially lenient and his connections will have the option of targeting a valuable pot or two before his sights are raised again somewhere down the line. **Alan King**

Conclusion: *Developed into a smart novice hurdler last season and often shaped as if longer trips are worth exploring; will stay 3m*

Our Power (Ire)   c143

7 b.g. Power – Scripture (Ire) (Sadler's Wells (USA))
2021/22 c18d⁵ c20.2d* c20.5sᶠ c19.9v* c24d³ c25g⁵ Mar 15

Cheltenham Gold Cup-winning jockey Sam Thomas has been steadily improving his numbers since switching to the training ranks and the latest campaign was the first in which he saddled over 100 runners. The £490,000 he amassed in total prize money beat his previous-best haul by over £300,000 and he celebrated big-race wins at Ascot for principal owner Dai Walters courtesy of Before Midnight and Good Risk At All, while Stolen Silver landed an all-important Cheltenham victory, albeit a month after the Festival.

Thomas' biggest success of the season was with Iwilldoit—owned by Diamond Racing Ltd—in the Welsh Grand National at Chepstow. Iwilldoit could be a potential Aintree contender this season, while Thomas is also likely to have big ambitions for another Walters-owned horse in the shape of Our Power, who came a long way in just six starts over fences in 2021/22.

Our Power was immediately thrown into handicap company for his chasing debut at Kempton in November where mistakes blighted his challenge, ultimately passing the post seven lengths behind the winner in fifth. However, he showed the benefit of that experience when going on to win two of his next three starts in small fields, showing a good attitude to land novice limited handicaps at Wincanton and Huntingdon either side of a first fence fall at Doncaster.

Our Power had much stiffer tasks ahead of him, but he shaped encouragingly both when third in the Coral Trophy Handicap Chase back at Kempton in February and fifth in the Ultima Handicap Chase at the Cheltenham Festival the following month. He was beaten eight lengths at Kempton and looked unlucky not to finish closer still given that he met trouble and pecked at the last, while his effort at Cheltenham could also be marked up, forced to race wide throughout and doing well to finish just outside the places having looked likely to fall back down the field turning in.

There is an air of unfinished business about Our Power after those two runs and he is clearly a well-handicapped horse given that he was 2 lb out of the weights at Cheltenham. Both his wins last season came over two and a half miles, but he stays much better than one might expect from one with his Flat pedigree, doing his best work at the finish over three miles at Kempton. That versatility with regards trip will give him plenty of options this season and there could be a big handicap with his name on it for his up-and-coming handler. *Sam Thomas*

Conclusion: Held his own in two fiercely competitive handicap chases last season despite not being seen to best effect, shaping like a horse who is still ahead of the handicapper

---

Rafferty's Return   h120+
7 b.g. Schiaparelli (Ger) – Duchess Theatre (Ire) (King's Theatre (Ire))
2021/22 h20.3s* h19.7d² h19.7v* h22g⁴ Mar 19

Physique is an obvious starting point when identifying which horses will thrive for the switch to fences—a big, rangy gelding will typically have more scope for improvement than a neat, smaller sort—but hurdling technique can also be indicative.

Rafferty's Return fits the bill on both counts being a tall type who took the eye with how fluently he jumped during his novice hurdling campaign, and that accuracy bodes well for his prospects over fences, where precise jumping takes on even greater importance.

Rafferty's Return made a winning start over hurdles at Newcastle where he opened up a big advantage after striding on over a circuit out and, aided by fluent jumping, never looked like being reeled in. That four-and-a-half-length success may have been achieved in slightly unconventional fashion, but the winning time suggested that Rafferty's Return wasn't flattered and, indeed, was deserving of credit for keeping up the gallop after taking a strong hold in the early stages.

Rafferty's Return had to settle for second on his next outing at Wetherby, where he was only denied by another promising sort and pulled well clear of the third, but it wasn't long before he struck again. Back at Wetherby, contesting what looked like an above-average novice for the North, Rafferty's Return registered a five-length success over the market leader who had some useful graded form to his name. As at Newcastle, Rafferty's Return put in a sure-footed round of jumping and impressed with how he maintained a good gallop on testing ground.

Conditions were quicker when Rafferty's Return disappointed at Newcastle having been sent off an odds-on favourite on his handicap debut, and it's possible he will be seen to best effect when there's plenty of cut in the ground. The step up in trip to two and three-quarter miles (raced previously at around two and a half miles) perhaps didn't suit such an enthusiastic sort either, while it may simply have been a flat performance on the back of three big efforts. Whatever the reason for the flop, Rafferty's Return had created such a good impression on his previous outings that he is well worth another chance. *Rebecca Menzies*

Conclusion: *Caught the eye with how fluently he jumped during a novice hurdling campaign which yielded a couple of wins; appeals as the type who will take well to chasing and his effectiveness on testing ground will be an asset during the winter months*

Red Rookie   c141
7 ch.g. Black Sam Bellamy (Ire) – Auction Belle (Auction House (USA))
2021/22 c16d² c16.8dF c16s* c15.9gF Mar 15

It's fair to say that star staying hurdler Paisley Park has elevated Emma Lavelle's status in the training ranks in recent seasons, though he hasn't lacked for a supporting cast either. Indeed, Lavelle has also plundered some of the most prestigious handicaps in the National Hunt calendar since Paisley Park began his climb through the ranks, including the Ladbrokes Trophy with De Rasher Counter, the Lanzarote Hurdle with Boreham Bill and the Classic Chase with Éclair Surf.

A higher level than a heritage handicap was the final port of call for Red Rookie last season, as he took part in the Sporting Life Arkle Challenge Trophy Novices' Chase at the Cheltenham Festival, the 80/1 chance still going well three out before he came under pressure and fell at the last. He ended the season with a BHA mark of 140 and certainly showed enough to suggest he can be placed to advantage by his shrewd handler off that rating.

Placed in a point before joining Lavelle, Red Rookie is still lightly raced full stop and his run in the Arkle was just the ninth of his career under Rules. His novice chasing season pre-Cheltenham was made up of a second in a novice limited handicap at Chepstow in November, a fall when going well in a similar event at Ascot the following month and a convincing novice chase win at Hereford early in the new year. He set a good standard on the last occasion and didn't need to improve to open his account over fences, leading before the last and just needing to be driven out from there to win by three and a quarter lengths.

Red Rookie might have fallen in two of his four starts over fences to date, but he is essentially a good jumper and has a physique (big gelding) which suggests his best days could still be ahead of him as he fills into his frame. A pacy sort, he may prove best at around two miles and will have options throughout the season having proved his effectiveness on ground ranging from good to heavy. He can pay his way in the top two-mile handicap chases, with all roads surely leading to the Grand Annual. ***Emma Lavelle***

Conclusion: *Just one win to show for a promising first season over fences but should be adding to his tally sooner rather than later; one to look out for in the big handicap chases at around 2m*

Richmond Lake (Ire) h132

6 b.g. Westerner – Chic Milan (Ire) (Milan)

2021/22 h16.7s* h17v^3 h19.9v* h15.7s^2 h18.1s^F h16.5g Apr 8

Switched from Eugene O'Sullivan to Donald McCain after just one run in a Punchestown bumper in the spring of 2021, Richmond Lake made a very promising start to life with his new yard last season, winning two of his six starts despite still looking far from the finished article.

Strong in the betting returning from eight months off, Richmond Lake was able to make a successful hurdling debut in the manner of a good prospect at Bangor in November, readily accounting for one who had himself made a very favourable impression first time up. After racing with enthusiasm at the head of affairs, he quickened clear approaching two out and just needed to be kept up to his work from there to win by 15 lengths.

Richmond Lake could only match that form when faced with testing conditions at Aintree next time, again trying to make all but cut down close home by both North Lodge and Bombs Away. He was then upped in trip at Sedgefield on Boxing Day and made the most of a simple opportunity—he returned an SP of 7/1-on—to get his head back in front, drawing clear from the home turn to win unchallenged by 27 lengths.

Richmond Lake looked well worth a try at a higher level and ran probably his best race when taking on graded company for the first time in the Sky Bet Supreme Trial Rossington Main Novices' Hurdle at Haydock in January. The star act there was Jonbon, but he was given a scare by Richmond Lake, who made the running back over two miles and briefly looked to have his rival in trouble before Nicky Henderson's charge finally asserted after the last to win by three lengths.

Though Richmond Lake won over two and a half miles at Sedgefield, he generally left the impression that two miles is likely to prove his optimum trip, most notably when he ran in the Premier Novices' Hurdle over two and a quarter miles at Kelso in March. He was full of beans as ever and looked the likeliest winner when quickening from two out, but his stamina ebbed away late on and he was already starting to weaken when crumpling to the floor on landing at the last.

Too free when down the field on his handicap debut at Aintree in April, Richmond Lake clearly has plenty to learn, but it's testament to his raw talent that he still achieved a useful level of form over hurdles. Crucially, he promises to be at least as good over fences this season, a good-topped gelding who made the frame on the last of his three starts in Irish points. *Donald McCain*

Conclusion: *Showed useful form despite doing plenty wrong over hurdles and has smart novice chaser written all over him for this season; may prove best at around 2m*

Serious Charges (Ire) h130

5 b.g. Soldier of Fortune (Ire) – South West Nine (Ire) (Oscar (Ire))
2021/22 b16d^2 h16.7s* h21.7s* h23.3s* h24.7d^6 Apr 9

Anthony Honeyball is a trainer who does especially well in bumpers and Serious Charges made a very promising start to his career under Rules when filling the runner-up spot behind a previous winner at Chepstow in December. However, a £85,000 purchase after finishing second on his sole start in Irish points, who is related to winners over hurdles, his future was always going to lie over obstacles, and he duly opened his account in good style in a two-mile maiden hurdle at Exeter 45 days later.

Serious Charges beat a couple of other interesting hurdling debutants with a bit to spare on that occasion, just needing be kept up to his work to assert in the closing stages, ultimately winning by three and three-quarter lengths. He didn't need to improve to follow up under a penalty in a weak novice hurdle at Fontwell next time, given a positive ride despite stepping up five furlongs in trip and well on top at the line despite making a mistake at the final flight.

The handicapper took a lenient view of his form and Serious Charges made a mockery of his opening mark of 120 when completing a hat-trick at Uttoxeter in March, pulling six lengths clear of another handicap debut who in turn was 16 lengths clear of the third in what probably wasn't the strongest race of its type. Still, it was hard not to be impressed by the manner of his victory, always travelling powerfully up even further in trip and also showing improvement in the jumping department.

Serious Charges then started favourite for a Grade 3 handicap at Aintree's Grand National meeting, but that was where his winning run came to an end, perhaps finding a better handicap in a bigger field a bit of a shock to the system. He did at least beat many more than beat him, though, finishing sixth of the 21 runners, and that experience will have done him no harm in the long run.

Very much a chasing type on looks, Serious Charges has certainly laid some solid foundations with a view to going over fences, particularly for one so young (still only a five-year-old). He is likely to rate even higher in that sphere and his connections can look forward to another productive campaign with him in novice handicap chases.
Anthony Honeyball

Conclusion: *Progressed well over hurdles and has the physique to develop into an even better chaser from what still looks a lenient mark*

Shan Blue (Ire) c159

8 b.g. Shantou (USA) – Lady Roberta (Ire) (Bob Back (USA))
2021/22 c24.2d^F c20.6d^6 c25d^2 Apr 9

Pause the replay of the Charlie Hall Chase at Wetherby last October on the approach to three out and Shan Blue was in the process of delivering one of the most visually striking performances in the race's recent history. Put simply, the way he moved to the front and then put around 22 lengths between himself and the chasing pack, seemingly in a matter of strides, was staggering. So was the sense of shock when, for one of the first times in his young chasing career, he made a mistake, taking off too far from the fence and hitting the deck.

The Skeltons had seen a big prize slip from their gasp and then a week later came the news that Shan Blue was stiff in his neck and would be on the sidelines for the foreseeable future. In fact, he wasn't to be seen on the track again until the Cheltenham Festival where he lined up for the Ryanair Chase as the shortest-priced British contender at 10/1. But the spark of Wetherby was missing in those deeper waters as Shan Blue travelled strongly until being brushed aside by the Irish armada off the home turn, ultimately passing the post 32 lengths behind Allaho.

Shan Blue's sights were lowered at Aintree's Grand National meeting, with connections opting to try and take advantage of a BHA mark of 148 by contesting the Grade 3 Betway Handicap Chase. For a horse who'd looked a potential mid-160s chaser at Wetherby, it's easy to see why they dipped their toes in the handicap waters and you'd expect them to return there this season after his Merseyside run. Though ultimately proving no match for Sam Brown on that occasion, he still shaped like one who had been let in lightly, impressing with how easily he made headway mid-race and perhaps just getting to the front earlier than ideal before he was swept aside by the winner from two out.

Beaten 15 lengths at the line, Shan Blue pulled another 10 lengths clear of the remainder and that appeals as solid handicap form, all of which suggests he remains one to be positive about from an unchanged mark heading into this season. He is effective at three miles but isn't short of speed, with the Paddy Power Gold Cup appealing as an ideal early-season target. *Dan Skelton*

Conclusion: *Very smart chaser who is on a lenient mark and looks up to landing a valuable handicap before returning to graded company*

Skytastic (Fr) h130p

6 b.g. Way of Light (USA) – Verzasca (Ire) (Sadler's Wells (USA))
2021/22 h19.4d* h19.3v* h24.7g Apr 8

Like stablemate and fellow *Fifty* member Our Power, Skytastic is bred more for the Flat than he is a career over jumps. He is by Way of Light, a smart performer in France when trained by Pascal Bary, notably winning the 1998 Grand Criterium, while his dam Verzasca is a daughter of Sadler's Wells who won on the level herself. For good measure, Skytastic is also a sibling to no fewer than eight winners on the Flat, including the useful Val d'Hiver.

Skytastic probably could have fashioned a career for himself on the Flat given the speed he showed when winning both his starts in bumpers in 2020/21, but instead he was sent novice hurdling last season, making his debut in a maiden over two and a half miles at Doncaster in January. His jumping there was notably assured for a debutant as he maintained his unbeaten record, winning by three and three-quarter lengths and looking value for extra having mastered the long-time leader, fellow *Fifty* member Godrevy Point, from three out. The timefigure also suggested Skytastic was full value for a fairly useful effort, with the promise of more to come.

Next up was a novice hurdle at Ascot three weeks later, a useful contest won by the likes of Dashel Drasher (2019) and Sporting John (2020) in recent years. Sent off the 6/5 favourite, Skytastic duly took another step forward to defy his penalty, hitting the front approaching two out and finding plenty when joined soon after to get the verdict by a neck. Incidentally, the time of that race stood up well to that of his smart stable companion Good Risk At All, who won a handicap over the same course and distance later on the card.

Skytastic (right) has the physique to take well to chasing

Skytastic had certainly shown enough to suggest he was worth his place at a higher level and his opportunity came at Aintree's Grand National meeting where he was stepped up to three miles for the Sefton Novices' Hurdle. He was one of the leading contenders in the betting and everything appeared to be going to plan on the approach to three out, still travelling well and holding every chance at the time. However, a bad mistake there put him on the back foot and he was simply unable to recover, ultimately trailing in down the field.

Skytastic is best not judged too harshly on that run and his best days are surely still ahead of him given how few miles he has on the clock. A big, good-topped gelding, he has the potential to take high rank as a novice chaser this season, sure to progress and win more races. **Sam Thomas**

Conclusion: *Lightly raced six-year-old who showed plenty of ability over hurdles last season and has the physique and demeanour to develop into an even better chaser*

Sonigino (Fr) h121

5 b.g. It's Gino (Ger) – Soniador (Fr) (Legolas (Jpn))
2021/22 h17.4s* h17.4s* h15.7g³ h16.6d⁵ h19.3s⁴ h16.3d⁵ h18.5s⁵ Mar 22

Recruiting horses from France is a tried-and-tested avenue for Paul Nicholls—think Kauto Star, Master Minded and Big Buck's—and, though Sonigino is yet to win a race in Britain, he has shown bits and pieces of form which make him a horse to be positive about.

Sonigino won twice over hurdles for David Cottin in his native France, wearing a tongue strap on both occasions, but that equipment was left off for his British debut in a listed novice hurdle at Haydock in November. He shaped encouragingly on that occasion, passing the post five lengths behind the useful winner, Barrichello, and leaving the impression the run would bring him on after five months off. He also impressed with his overall physique, a rangy, athletic sort who moved well, displaying all the hallmarks of a future chaser.

Admittedly, Sonigino didn't progress as expected on his next couple of starts, simply running poorly on his handicap debut at Doncaster in December and then pulling too hard when stepped up to two and a half miles at Ascot in January when refitted with a tongue strap. He fared better back in novice company under a double penalty at Newbury in February, but that was at a time when the Nicholls yard was under a cloud and his finishing effort reflected that after he had travelled strongly into contention.

Sonigino was last seen in a handicap hurdle at Exeter in March where he was again below form, finding little having typically taken a strong hold. It was essentially a frustrating first season with his new yard, though it wouldn't be the biggest surprise if it proves a different story when he goes chasing this season.

In a recent stable tour, Nicholls reported that Sonigino had been struggling with his wind, so he has undergone a breathing operation since last seen (not uncommon for one from this yard) and it was confirmed that the plan is to go chasing. He will start life over fences from what looks a lenient BHA mark of 119 based on the pick of his form over hurdles, appealing as very much one to keep on the right side in novice handicap chases at up to two and a half miles. **Paul Nicholls**

Conclusion: Showed ability over hurdles but has chaser written all over him and looks a good prospect for novice handicaps over fences from his lowly mark

Sounds Russian (Ire)   c148

7 b.g. Sholokhov (Ire) – Reevolesa (Ire) (Revoque (Ire))
2021/22 h20.4g² h20.4s² h20.1s² c19.3d⁴ c21.1s* c22.3v* c23.4v* c24.1g² Apr 2

A good type physically and highly likely to improve with another summer under his belt, Sounds Russian has already come a long way in a short space of time. He filled the runner-up spot in his three starts over hurdles before being pitched straight into a handicap on his chasing debut at Sedgefield in November. That was a run full of promise as he passed the post less than four lengths behind the winner, making good late gains under considerate handling, his rider sticking to just hands-and-heels riding as he still looked green under pressure.

It didn't take Sounds Russian long to leave that form behind and there was no stopping him once he found the winning groove, going on to complete a hat-trick of victories by a cumulative margin of 48 lengths. After winning at Sedgefield and Kelso, both in December, Sounds Russian then returned to the last-named venue in February from a 21 lb higher mark than when he started his chasing career. He tended to go slightly right at his fences but was always going best and had the race in safe keeping after a good jump three out, ultimately winning unchallenged by 22 lengths.

Sounds Russian had his winning ended when last seen contesting a valuable novice handicap chase at Ayr's Scottish Grand National meeting, but he ran another cracker in defeat. He led briefly after the last and hit the basement price of 1.01 in-running on the Betfair Exchange, but the smart Dusart (who also features in the *Fifty*) just edged him out close home to land the spoils by half a length, with the pair pulling clear of the rest.

Sounds Russian ran from a BHA mark of 145 at Ayr and starts the new campaign on 150. That still leaves him with a bit of room for manouevre, particularly as it's easy to foresee further progress considering how much he's improved in just eight races so far. He looks set to be a fixture in the valuable staying handicap chases in the North. **Ruth Jefferson**

Conclusion: Most progressive over fences last season and looks an ideal type for the big staying handicaps in the North this term

Strong Leader   b105p

5 b.g. Passing Glance – Strong Westerner (Ire) (Westerner)
2021/22 NR :: 2022/23 b16g* May 7

Here's a horse who is firmly in the could-be-anything category. Strong Leader has made just the one appearance so far, but he was so dominant when winning his bumper at Warwick in May that we simply couldn't leave him out of our *Fifty*.

A rangy, chasing type, Strong Leader very much caught the eye in the preliminaries and was even more impressive in the race itself. Sent off the 3/1 second favourite, he was patiently ridden by Adrian Heskin and made smooth headway out of the back straight. There was a moment shortly after turning in when he showed understandable greenness, but he was very quick to learn, going through the gears to lead under two furlongs out and finishing with rare speed from there to shoot clear of his rivals. The official winning margin was seven and a half lengths and it was noticeable just how long it took Heskin to pull him up afterwards.

Strong Leader is by Passing Glance and out of Strong Westerner, who is herself a half-sister to the high-class staying chaser Strong Flow. That makes him a brother to the quirky Strong Glance, whose future once looked just as bright after he'd won two of his three starts in bumpers for the same connections. However, his temperament has been an issue more recently, achieving a fairly useful level of form over hurdles but also having the Timeform squiggle attached to his rating to denote that he is not one to trust.

So, Strong Leader needs to prove he has superior resolution to his sibling but, in terms of raw ability and physique, he couldn't have created a bigger impression at Warwick. An exciting prospect, he will be one to look out for in the novice hurdling ranks this season.
Olly Murphy

Conclusion: *Looked potentially something out of the ordinary when making a winning debut in a Warwick bumper and appeals as one of the more interesting recruits to the British novice hurdling ranks this season*

Thanksforthehelp (Fr)   h117p

5 gr.g. Martaline – Agathe du Berlais (Fr) (Poliglote)
2021/22 b15.8g⁴ h16s³ h15.8v² h15.2g² :: 2022/23 h19.8d³ Apr 27

David Pipe has enjoyed a good start to the 2022/23 National Hunt season, already well on course to smash last term's tally of winners out of the water, and Thanksforthehelp is just the sort of horse who can rack up a sequence in handicap hurdles from what looks a lenient mark.

Thanksforthehelp is bred to be smart—his dam is a half-sister to the high-class hurdler Agrapart—and he caught the eye on more than one occasion last season, shaping much better than the bare result on his debut in a bumper at Southwell before showing ability in four starts over hurdles.

Thanksforthehelp had a breathing operation after his debut and was given a considerate introduction over hurdles when third in a novice event at Chepstow in December, failing to settle early and making some novicey mistakes but shaping well by the end of the race. On his next start at Huntingdon he again shaped like a horse with ability when finishing runner-up, and he left a similar impression when filling the same position in another novice at Wincanton where he did well to make the odds-on favourite work hard given that rival was able to dictate a steady pace.

Pitched straight into a fiercely competitive heat at the Punchestown Festival for his handicap debut, Thanksforthehelp was sent off the 7/2 favourite and went through that race like a horse ahead of his mark in a first-time tongue strap. That was his first start beyond two miles and he briefly looked the likeliest winner when looming up on the home turn. However, he simply didn't see out the longer trip quite as well as the first two, with a couple of later errors not helping his cause either as he passed the post two and a half lengths behind the winner. The form of that race looks solid and Thanksforthehelp is almost certainly a well-handicapped horse entering this season. He remains a maiden, so his novice status is still intact, and he has the profile of one who could mop up some novice handicaps from his lowly mark. **David Pipe**

Conclusion: *Lightly raced hurdler who figures on a good mark and is very much unexposed; has the potential to rack up a sequence*

Tile Tapper   c126p

8 b.g. Malinas (Ger) – Darn Hot (Sir Harry Lewis (USA))
2021/22 h19.5m c19.2s⁴ c20s c19.4s* Feb 26

In his first three starts last season, Tile Tapper was beaten by a cumulative margin of 135 lengths, arguably looking the furthest thing from a horse to follow at that stage of his career. But then he went to Chepstow in February and changed all that, winning in the style of a horse with more to offer and very much earning his place in our *Fifty*.

Winner of a bumper at Exeter on New Year's Day in 2020, Tile Tapper never tasted success over timber but kept good company, including on last season's reappearance when he lined up in the Grade 2 Persian War Novices' Hurdle at Chepstow. That looked a stiff task on paper and so it proved as he tracked the pace before dropping away early in the straight, eventually finishing last of the seven runners behind Camprond.

Chasing always looked like being Tile Tapper's game and he was switched to the larger obstacles at Exeter when next seen in December. Connections opted to go down the handicap route from a BHA mark of 121 and he was strong in the market beforehand but never really looked like justifying the confidence after making several mistakes. While in contention down the back straight, he gradually lost touch from the fourth last and was beaten a total of 24 lengths at the line. Tile Tapper was again well backed when making his next appearance at Lingfield's Winter Millions fixture in January, but he did nothing in the race to give his supporters any cause for optimism. It was another catalogue of errors, literally, though an excuse for his below-par showing did at least come to light subsequently as he was reported to have bled.

Thankfully, there were no signs of that physical issue at Chepstow where Tile Tapper put it all together for the first time over fences, improving on even his best form over hurdles. He travelled well and jumped soundly throughout, always looking in control after quickening to lead approaching three out. He idled in front but still won readily by seven and a half lengths in a race which is proving strong form—the third Black Gerry, who was beaten a total of nine lengths, has won two of his three starts since.

That suggests Tile Tapper is still a well-handicapped horse from a BHA mark of 124, particularly when you factor in his scope for more improvement after just three starts over fences. He missed the spring but is reportedly back in training with Chris Honour and can hopefully pick up where he left off at the end of last season. **Chris Honour**

Conclusion: *Finally put it all together when getting off the mark over fences at Chepstow and should win more races with further progress on the cards*

Tim Pat (Ire)   c123p
6 b.g. Mahler – April Thyne (Ire) (Presenting)
2021/22 h16.2d h15.8v⁵ h19.9s³ h23.3v² h24.1s² h23s* c20d* c28.4m* Mar 23

2021/22 h16.2d h15.8v^5 h19.9s^3 h23.3v^2 h24.1s^2 h23s* c20d* c28.4m* Mar 23

Donald McCain enjoyed more winners (155) than any other National Hunt trainer in Britain last season, while his strike rate of 23% was arguably just as impressive. Crucially, it was also the first time McCain had saddled more than 100 winners in a season since 2013/14, but it's unlikely that he'll have to wait so long to repeat that feat given that he already has 41 winners on the board in 2022/23 at the time of writing.

Tim Pat is one of three horses from the McCain yard in this year's *Fifty* who look set to provide the stable with further success. It took Tim Pat six attempts to break his duck last term, but he was well on top when eventually opening his account in a handicap hurdle at Bangor in February. Held up in the early stages, he travelled smoothly throughout and gradually asserted after being produced to lead at the second last, just needing to be pushed out on the run-in to win by two and a quarter lengths with a bit to spare.

Tim Pat is every inch a chaser on looks and duly showed improved form to make the perfect start over fences in a handicap chase at Carlisle later in February, seeing it out thoroughly back down in trip to two and a half miles. He made headway under pressure three out and was in front going to the last before Theo Gillard was able to ease him down close home to land the spoils by four and a quarter lengths.

That performance earned Tim Pat an 8 lb rise in the weights, but he overcame that—and a marked step up in trip to three and a half miles—to make it two from two as a chaser at

Haydock in March. The official winning margin there was just a length, but he was value for extra having been asked to do little more than necessary to master the pacesetter after the last.

That win came on going described by Timeform as good to firm, but he's already proven in the mud as well. He has also proved his effectiveness over a wide range of trips, demonstrating versatility which will give him plenty of options this season. He is still low mileage over fences and couldn't be in better hands to enjoy another productive campaign. **Donald McCain**

Conclusion: *Unbeaten in two starts over fences and looks sure to go on improving this season when he'll have plenty of options given his versatility with regards conditions*

Unexpected Party (Fr)   h138
7 gr.g. Martaline – Reform Act (USA) (Lemon Drop Kid (USA))
2021/22 h16.7d⁴ h21.3d* h21d² h21.3v² h19.3s* h21sᵖᵘ Mar 16

Unexpected Party improved in leaps and bounds as a hurdler last winter, earning himself a tilt at the Coral Cup at the Cheltenham Festival in March. In the event, it didn't happen for him in the deeper waters of the Festival where he stopped quite quickly after three out and was pulled up. He's sure to bounce back before too long, though, and it's worth revisiting what he did in his first five starts last season to warrant his place in the *Fifty*.

Unexpected Party is clear of his rivals at Ascot

After filling the runner-up spot on his debut in a maiden hurdle at Southwell in September 2020, Unexpected Party reappeared just over 12 months later in a similar event at Bangor where he weakened into fourth having taken a strong hold. That at least qualified him for handicaps and his connections didn't waste any time exploiting an opening BHA mark of 103 as he headed north to Wetherby a month later. Upped in trip to two miles and five furlongs, he essentially proved himself to be some way ahead of the handicapper, leading on the bridle two out and quickly forging clear from there to win by eight lengths with any amount in hand.

That performance earned Unexpected Party an 11 lb hike in the weights, but he looked like defying his new mark for a long way when making his next appearance in a valuable handicap hurdle at Cheltenham's November meeting. He was beaten only two and half lengths after conceding first run to the winner, Gowel Road, though it probably didn't make a difference to the result as he wasn't quite so strong in the finish as that rival anyway.

Back in calmer waters at Wetherby on Boxing Day, Unexpected Party was sent off the 13/8-on favourite to resume winning ways and everything appeared to be going to plan until he hit the brakes at the last when at least three lengths clear. He picked up again, but the damage had already been done as his late rally could only get him back within a length of the winner.

Up to a mark of 130 after that, Unexpected Party quickly gained compensation with a striking win in the Holloway's Handicap Hurdle at Ascot in January, winning by four and a half lengths and looking value for extra having been eased close home. Put a line through his Coral Cup run and this strong-travelling sort remains very much one for the shortlist in valuable handicaps, including over fences should his connections choose to pursue that route. **Dan Skelton**

Conclusion: *Proved most progressive prior to his Cheltenham blip and doesn't look handicapped out of things from a BHA mark of 141, particularly with a view to going chasing*

West Cork   h144
8 b.g. Midnight Legend – Calamintha (Mtoto)
2021/22 h16.4g* h15.7d⁵ h16.8d⁴ h16g² :: 2022/23 h15.7dᶠ May 7

If you need persuading about Dan Skelton's skills as a trainer, and fewer and fewer people do, then West Cork's win in last season's Greatwood Hurdle is probably 'Exhibit A'. Having spent 631 days on the sidelines prior to that, West Cork somehow returned razor-sharp for his handicap debut in the cauldron of Cheltenham's November meeting, shrugging off his absence and any fears over a lack of experience to beat Adagio three quarters of a length despite his jockey dropping his whip at the last.

The Betfair Exchange Trophy at Ascot was the next port of call, but he failed to hit the same heights, with more holding ground on the back of a much shorter break perhaps just taking the edge off his finishing effort after he'd looked a danger to all. He was beaten a total of 16 lengths behind Tritonic—who had finished behind him in the Greatwood—but any notion that he couldn't be competitive from a 7 lb higher mark was quickly dispelled in the spring.

Three months later West Cork got right back on track when finishing fourth behind State Man in the County Hurdle at the Cheltenham Festival, showing form at least as good as when winning the Greatwood. Held up in the early stages, he made good headway to chase the leaders at the last and kept on well from there to pass the post only five lengths behind the winner.

West Cork still had a couple of big two-mile handicap hurdles on his agenda in the spring, taking his racing particularly well given how long he'd spent off the track before last season. He first filled the runner-up spot in the Scottish Champion Hurdle at Ayr, edging ahead in the final 100 yards only to prove vulnerable to the winner's late surge, and then fell three out when in the process of running well in the Swinton Handicap Hurdle at Haydock, though it's hard to say where he would have finished.

West Cork will begin this season on a BHA mark of 144 and there is no reason why he shouldn't remain competitive in good handicap hurdles. However, he arguably has the ingredients of an even better chaser, a well-made winning pointer by Midnight Legend. Perhaps he will plot a similar path to the same owner's Third Time Lucki, who achieved a smart level of form when running in most of the big two-mile novice chases in Britain last season. **Dan Skelton**

Conclusion: *Made good strides last season after returning a long absence and possibly now or never for a chasing career given his age; has the tools to develop into a smart novice over fences at up to 2½m*

Weveallbeencaught (Ire)   b104

5 b.g. Getaway (Ger) – Curvacious (Ire) (Anshan)
2021/22 b16.3s* Mar 5

The bumper on the Greatwood Gold Cup card at Newbury in March only has a short history, but it's clearly a race to watch closely based on the limited evidence we have so far.

Indeed, it already has a more decorated roll of honour than many similar events which have been going much longer, with Sam Brown (2017) and McFabulous (2019) featuring among the winners from just four runnings. Sam Brown is now well established as a very smart chaser for Anthony Honeyball and was last seen running out an impressive 15-length winner of a valuable handicap chase at Aintree's Grand National meeting, while McFabulous also ended last season on a high, gaining the fourth Grade 2 success of his career with a smart performance in the Select Hurdle at Sandown.

Big shoes to fill then for the 2022 winner Weveallbeencaught, but there was nothing about the manner of his debut victory to suggest that he doesn't have a very bright future in his own right. Bought for £210,000 after winning an Irish point in December, Weveallbeencaught is bred more for stamina than speed and has a big, powerful physique, so it was really encouraging that he could win at Newbury given the way things developed. In a race run at just an ordinary gallop, he took a keen hold in rear in the early stages and needed to be ridden entering the straight. It took him a while to find his stride, but there was plenty to like about the way he stayed on to assert close home, ultimately winning by half a length from Collectors Item, with the pair of previous winners in third and fourth giving substance to the form.

It was certainly an encouraging start to Weveallbeencaught's career under Rules and, likely to prove best when the emphasis is more on stamina, he must be considered an exciting prospect for novice hurdles over two and a half miles and beyond this season. Incidentally, Twiston-Davies seemingly has grander plans than those, long-term, likening Weveallbeencaught to Imperial Commander and saying he was bought as a Gold Cup horse. If his trainer is right, this fellow could take some catching wherever he goes this season. **Nigel Twiston-Davies**

Conclusion: *Overcame adverse circumstances to win a Newbury bumper on his debut under Rules and looks a smart staying prospect for novice hurdles with that experience under his belt*

SECTION

2

Ain't That A Shame (Ire) c146

8 b.g. Jeremy (USA) – Castletown Girl (Bob Back (USA))
2021/22 c21s³ c21s² c24s² c26d Mar 17

Ain't That A Shame perhaps doesn't have the same amount of quality as some of the top-notchers at the Henry de Bromhead yard, but he has some smart form to his name and strikes as the type who is up to winning a top-end handicap over fences this season.

A runner-up on his sole start in Irish points, Ain't That A Shame's future was always going to lie over fences and he made a promising start to life in that sphere when bumping into a couple of the top novice chasers from last season. He was a bit too keen on his return from 10 months off when 15 lengths third to Stattler on his chasing debut at Fairyhouse in December, though shaped with plenty of promise, and was then unlucky to run into the very exciting Galopin des Champs, who dismissed him by 22 lengths, on his next start at Leopardstown later in December. Those rivals both went on to win in graded company last season and will have Gold Cup aspirations this time round.

Ain't That A Shame was strong in the betting at Navan next time and was very unfortunate not to open his account over fences, going clear between the last two and looking to be in full control (traded at 1.03 in-running on the Betfair Exchange) before hanging to his left on the run-in and leaving the door open for one who finished with a flourish. He was then handed a lenient-looking opening mark and started second favourite for the Kim Muir at the Cheltenham Festival on his final start, but he produced a disappointing effort, coming home last of the 13 finishers and looking extremely tired in the straight. He was too buzzed up in the early stages to do himself justice and it is probably best to ignore that run.

Ain't That A Shame still has his novice status over fences intact heading into this season and, based on his early form in this sphere, he is very much a horse to keep on the right side from a mark of 137, sure to be competitive in some of the better staying handicaps in Ireland. **Henry De Bromhead**

Conclusion: *Unexposed staying chaser who is potentially well handicapped and has the potential to pick up a big pot this season*

Ashroe Diamond (Ire) b109

5 b.m. Walk In The Park (Ire) – Saine d'Esprit (Fr) (Dom Alco (Fr))
2021/22 b16v* b16.7g² b16s⁴ b17d* Apr 7

Willie Mullins took the first five editions of the Dawn Run Mares' Novices' Hurdle at the Cheltenham Festival and, while he has come up short in the last two renewals, there's no doubt his powerhouse yard remains the starting point when looking for the winner.

Patrick Mullins celebrates after guiding Ashroe Diamond to victory at Aintree

Grangee fared best of Mullins' sextet in the latest running, finishing third behind Love Envoi, the first British-trained winner of the race, but it could have been a different story had Brandy Love (another in the Irish list) not been ruled out on the morning of the race after she was found to be lame. Indeed, Brandy Love (h140p) ended the campaign as one of the highest-rated mares in the division after inflicting an eight-length defeat on Love Envoi when the pair clashed in the Grade 1 at Fairyhouse in April.

One who looks sure to take high rank in the division this time around is Ashroe Diamond, the pick of Mullins' mares in bumpers last season. Ashroe Diamond was out early, making her debut at Wexford in May, and she recorded an impressive success, cruising 14 lengths clear after travelling strongly. She then backed up that positive impression despite having to settle for second on her next outing at Galway, shaping well behind an older, much more experienced gelding.

Two of Ashroe Diamond's stablemates went off at a shorter price when she returned from six months off in the Grade 2 mares' bumper at the Dublin Racing Festival, but she fared best of the Mullins team in finishing a close-up fourth in a race that produced a blanket finish. She was then well backed for her final start of the campaign in the Grade 2 mares' bumper at Aintree, going off at 9/4, and her supporters wouldn't have had many anxious moments as she drew six lengths clear after tanking her way into contention.

By Timeform's reckoning that was the second best performance put up by a mare in a bumper last season—only the Nicky Henderson-trained Luccia earned a higher rating (b116)—and Ashroe Diamond, a mare by Walk In The Park out of a half-sister to the high-class chaser Quel Esprit, has the physique and pedigree to excel over jumps. **W. P. Mullins**

Conclusion: *One of the highest-rated mares in bumpers last season and ought to also develop into a leading player in novice hurdles restricted to her sex; likely type for the Dawn Run Mares' Novices' Hurdle at the Cheltenham Festival*

Brandy Love (Ire)   h140p
6 b.m. Jet Away – Bambootcha (Ire) (Saddlers' Hall (Ire))
2021/22 h15.8s* h18.5d² h20s* Apr 17

Prominent owner Mike Grech made the decision earlier this year to transfer all of his horses to Ireland due to him spending much more time in the country due to business commitments. He only had five horses based in Britain (four with Nicky Henderson and one with David Bridgewater), but it is still another hit for British National Hunt racing given how much Grech has spent at the sales in previous years—Henrietta Knight, who purchases most of Grech's horses, made a record-breaking £200,000 purchase at the Goffs UK Spring Store Sale at Doncaster in May.

Brandy Love herself was bought for £200,000 after winning her sole start in points and she looked a smart prospect when making a winning start under Rules in a bumper at Fairyhouse in December 2020. She also made a seamless transition to hurdling when landing the odds on her return in a mares' maiden at Naas last season, giving her backers a slight scare when making a bad mistake at the third flight but jumping well otherwise and easily stretching clear between the last two.

Brandy Love was again well supported to follow up in Grade 3 company at Fairyhouse on her next start and, while she didn't progress as expected, she did plenty wrong and arguably did well to be beaten only three and a half lengths behind useful stablemate Allegorie de Vassy. She raced clear of the field but showed a tendency to jump left—markedly so at times—and had already seen her advantage reduced when ploughing through the second last.

Despite that reversal, Brandy Love remained prominent in the betting for the Dawn Run Mares' Novices' Hurdle at the Cheltenham Festival before being ruled out due to a late setback. That race was won by Love Envoi, who then headed to Fairyhouse where she was emphatically put in her place by Brandy Love in the Irish Stallion Farms EBF Mares Novices' Hurdle Championship Final. That was an impressive performance from Brandy Love to prove herself a decidedly useful novice, once again jumping left at the final two flights but otherwise proving much more tractable fitted with a first-time hood. The step up to two and a half miles clearly brought out some improvement, too, as she forged clear on the run-in to win by eight lengths.

Brandy Love remains with plenty of potential after just three starts over hurdles and is expected to take her form to a new level this season, especially when switched back to a left-handed track. The Mares' Hurdle at the Cheltenham Festival—a race her trainer has a formidable record in—is sure to be one of her main targets. ***W. P. Mullins***

Conclusion: *Exciting prospect who will likely take plenty of beating in mares' events and looks tailormade for the Mares' Hurdle at the Cheltenham Festival*

Champ Kiely (Ire)   h127P

6 b.g. Ocovango – Cregg So (Ire) (Moscow Society (USA))
2021/22 b16v* :: 2022/23 h21g* Jul 27

Owner Margaret Masterson had her colours carried to one of the most impressive Cheltenham Festival victories of recent seasons when Appreciate It came home 24 lengths clear in the 2021 Supreme Novices' Hurdle. Without another run in the interim, Appreciate It didn't make the same impact when sent off second favourite for the Champion Hurdle, but he's also one of a trio of his owner's horses, along with Carefully Selected and Kilcruit, to have finished second in the Champion Bumper at the Festival in recent seasons, while Kilcruit also finished third in the latest Supreme.

Champ Kiely therefore has plenty to live up to in the blue and green diamond colours, but he has certainly made a very promising start to his career under Rules with Willie Mullins. He battled well to a half-length win in a bumper, in which the first two pulled well clear, on his debut at Limerick in May 2021, but it was then more than a year before he was seen on a racecourse again in a maiden hurdle at the latest Galway Festival. Champ Kiely looked an exciting prospect on that occasion, travelling powerfully and jumping accurately, and, having led with a circuit to go, drew clear from the home turn to win hard held by 21 lengths. Runner-up Esperti had already run to a fairly useful level, while the third, Dawn Rising, was sent off favourite for his hurdling debut after showing useful form on the Flat for Aidan O'Brien.

Champ Kiely, who unseated in his only start in points, has plenty of scope and will make a chaser in time, being a half-brother to Moscowsowhat, who was fairly useful over fences, as was his dam's half-brother Marufo. More immediately, though, he seems sure to prove worth following as he gains experience over hurdles. ***W. P. Mullins***

Conclusion: *Winner of both starts under Rules, including an impressive hurdling debut at the Galway Festival, for connections who are no strangers to unearthing Cheltenham Festival types*

El Fabiolo (Fr) h152

5 b.g. Spanish Moon (USA) – Sainte Mante (Fr) (Saint des Saints (Fr))
2021/22 h16v* h16.5g² :: 2022/23 h16d* Apr 29

Willie Mullins' now retired dual Gold Cup winner Al Boum Photo became a regular in Tramore's New Year's Day Chase and gained the final win of his career in the latest renewal of that contest when successful for a fourth time in January. But he wasn't always the stable's only good winner on that particular card. In 2020, Mullins won the two-mile maiden hurdle at Tramore with Saint Roi who, like Al Boum Photo that year, won at the Cheltenham Festival on his next start when landing some good bets in the County Hurdle. A very smart hurdler nowadays, Saint Roi was fourth in the latest Champion Hurdle.

Mullins also won the latest edition of that Tramore maiden with another French import, El Fabiolo, whose own future over jumps looks very bright. Sent off at very short odds on his first start for the yard at Tramore, El Fabiolo travelled strongly in the lead before drawing clear from two out for an impressive 13-length win over fairly useful stable companion Tempo Chapter Two. Typical of his trainer's patient approach with his recruits from France, El Fabiolo hadn't run for well over a year when making his Irish debut. He'd had just the two starts for Patricia Butel and Jean-Luc Beaunez, finishing down the field on the Flat but showing a lot more when third in a listed race for hurdling debutants at Auteuil.

El Fabiolo (left) is locked in battle with Jonbon at Aintree

El Fabiolo's lack of experience probably explained why he wasn't in his stable's Cheltenham Festival team, but he was highly tried next time out even so in the Top Novices' Hurdle at Aintree. Fitted with a hood this time, he had plenty to find beforehand to trouble the Supreme runner-up Jonbon but was sent off second favourite and made Nicky Henderson's winner work hard for his victory. Hampered three out and not fluent at the final flight, El Fabiolo kept on well nonetheless to challenge on the run-in and went down by just a neck with a gap of 19 length back to the third.

Without any headgear this time, El Fabiolo was found a perfect opportunity to go one better at the Punchestown Festival in a novice for horses who had not won more than once over hurdles, and he duly landed the odds readily by four lengths from stablemate Ha d'Or. Every inch a chaser on looks, El Fabiolo looks a cracking prospect for novices over fences this season. **W. P. Mullins**

Conclusion: *Lightly raced chasing type who made Jonbon pull out all the stops on his only try in Grade 1 company at Aintree and looks exciting for novice chases*

Fighter Allen (Fr)   c147p
7 b.g. Vision d'Etat (Fr) – Reaction (Fr) (Saint des Saints (Fr))
2021/22 h20.5d c21s² c21.3s⁴ c21.6d* :: 2022/23 c21dᶠ Apr 29

The EMS Copiers Novice Handicap Chase at the Punchestown Festival has been farmed by Willie Mullins in recent years. He has won six of the last seven renewals, including with Grade 1 winners Kemboy and Asterion Forlonge, and it's a race that has become a platform for talented performers.

Mullins won it again in 2022 with El Barra, but his number one hopeful going into the race was the 4/1 favourite, Fighter Allen, ridden by stable jockey Paul Townend. Fighter Allen was a casualty as early as the first fence, falling after jumping it well but landing steeply, but he remains a bright prospect. He also remains on a handicap mark of 144 over fences and that's a rating he could exploit in a handicap chase before moving into graded company. At Tramore, on his third chasing start, he certainly looked a steeplechaser of good ability, making all, travelling well and jumping fluently on his way to a comfortable six-length success.

With just four chasing starts under his belt, Fighter Allen has obvious potential to improve, his reputation at home underlined by the fact he was thrown into Grade 1 company on just his second start over fences at the Dublin Racing Festival at Leopardstown. Sent off at 66/1, he ended up being a modest 46-length fourth behind stable companion Galopin des Champs after being hampered at the sixth, briefly making headway three out but never threatening to get seriously involved faced with such a stiff task.

The experience clearly didn't do Fighter Allen any harm as he returned to the track nine weeks later to win at Tramore, while the less said about his subsequent appearance at

Punchestown the better. A brother to the multiple Grade 1 winner Envoi Allen, Fighter Allen can make his mark this season in chases at around two and a half miles, at first in handicap company before being tried at a higher level again. **W. P. Mullins**

Conclusion: *Achieved a smart level of form in his first season over fences and has plenty of options heading into 2022/23, on a good mark for handicaps and likely to progress further to make an impact in graded company*

Fil Dor (Fr)   h144
4 gr.g. Doctor Dino (Fr) – La Turbale (Fr) (Ange Gabriel (Fr))
2021/22 h16.9s* h16g* h16s* h16d² h16.8d² :: 2022/23 h16s² Apr 30

Gordon Elliott exploited the four-year-old allowance for chasers to great effect last season with Riviere d'Etel, who won three races over fences before Christmas and went on to push Ferny Hollow all the way in the Grade 1 Racing Post Novice Chase at Leopardstown on Boxing Day. Riviere d'Etel, of course, had a mares' allowance as well, but the significance of the age allowance shouldn't be underestimated, and her form dropped off later in the campaign when she didn't have it.

There are plenty of opportunities over fences for a good four-year-old before Christmas, though, and with that in mind Elliott could well plough a familiar furrow with Fil Dor, who achieved a higher level of form as a juvenile hurdler than Riviere d'Etel did before him. Fil Dor was one of the best in that division last season, notably winning his first three races over timber, including the Grade 2 Knight Frank Juvenile Hurdle, also on Leopardstown's Boxing Day card.

Fil Dor was then campaigned exclusively at the top level, starting with the Spring Juvenile Hurdle back at Leopardstown for the Dublin Racing Festival. He lost his unbeaten record there but ran at least as well as he had previously in finding only the Willie Mullins-trained Vauban too good, beating the rest comfortably but simply having no answer to the winner's superior turn of foot. It continued to be a similar story when the pair clashed again in both the Triumph Hurdle at the Cheltenham Festival and the Champion Four Year Old Hurdle at the Punchestown Festival. Frustratingly for his connections, Fil Dor ended the campaign with three second-place finishes at the top level to his name, with Vauban beating him each time by a cumulative margin of nine and a half lengths.

A listed winner on the Flat in France before joining Mullins, the speedy Vauban is likely to be on the Champion Hurdle trail this season, so at least Fil Dor will be able to avoid him when he goes novice chasing. A useful-looking gelding, Fil Dor is likely to stay two and a half miles and that will give him plenty of options with regards trip as he embarks on a career over fences. Crucially, his style of racing (front runner/races prominently) should lend itself well to chasing, while his runs over hurdles were often hallmarked by accurate jumping. As Elliott showed with Riviere d'Etel last season, Fil Dor couldn't be in better hands to enjoy another productive campaign. *Gordon Elliott*

Fil Dor (red cap) found only Vauban (pink) too good at Cheltenham

Conclusion: *Gained plenty of experience in juvenile hurdles last season and should be able to put that to good use in novice chases where he gets a healthy weight allowance; likely to stay 2½m*

Gerri Colombe (Fr)   h134p
6 b.g. Saddler Maker (Ire) – Ruse de Guerre (Fr) (Cadoudal (Fr))
2021/22 h20.2v* h23d* Jan 23

Gerri Colombe was not one of last season's highest-rated novice hurdlers, but that can be explained by a lack of opportunity rather than ability and, given the chance to show his true worth, it is expected he will take high rank among the novice chasers this term.

Gerri Colombe was bought for £240,000 after winning his only point for Colin Bowe and he could hardly have been more impressive on his debut under Rules for Gordon Elliott in January 2021. He landed that heavy-ground Fairyhouse bumper by 24 lengths, earning quotes of just 14/1 for the Champion Bumper, but Elliott was quick to play down talk of a trip to Cheltenham and instead highlighted the horse's long-term potential, stating: "He's probably going to be a big chaser more than anything, a big, staying horse down the road...I don't think you'll see a whole lot more of him this season, he might have one more run."

As suggested Gerri Colombe did indeed race only once more during his bumper campaign, posting a ready victory under a hands-and-heels ride at Naas which reinforced his status as a very smart prospect for jumping. Mindful of Elliott's "big chaser" comment, Gerri Colombe was always likely to be lightly raced over hurdles, but it was only an untimely setback in the weeks leading up to the Cheltenham Festival that meant his campaign was restricted to two starts in a Down Royal maiden and Thurles novice, both of which he won.

In contrast to his previous three wins under Rules, Gerri Colombe made his supporters sweat when landing the odds at Thurles, but, rather than denting his reputation, a gritty display around that tight, turning track on decent ground merely underlined his potential for improvement when faced with a sterner test of stamina.

There will be greater opportunities for this former pointer to encounter those stiff stamina tests over fences, and his proven ability to handle testing ground will be an asset over the winter months. With Gordon Elliott he is in excellent hands to fulfil his undoubted potential. **Gordon Elliott**

Conclusion: *Expensive recruit from the pointing ranks who remains unbeaten and looks the type to thrive over fences, particularly when faced with a stiff test of stamina (will be suited by 3m+)*

Life In The Park (Ire)   h132
5 b.g. Walk In The Park (Ire) – Jeanquiri (Fr) (Mansonnien (Fr))
2021/22 h21.7d³ h20s⁶ h20.3d* :: 2022/23 h19.8d* Apr 27

Barry Moloney won the Cheltenham Gold Cup in 2021 with Minella Indo just a year after his other top-class chaser Monalee finished a close fourth in the same race. It's asking a lot to expect the owner's Life In The Park to develop into a Gold Cup horse at this stage, as he's only a five-year-old and yet to run over fences, but the strong impression he gave in his first season over hurdles was that he's very much a staying chaser in the making.

Life In The Park looked a proper stayer right from his debut under Rules which came in a maiden hurdle at Punchestown where he got outpaced before rallying to finish six lengths third to the useful Freedom To Dream. Something was seemingly amiss in a similar event at Leopardstown just after Christmas, but Henry de Bromhead gave him plenty of time afterwards and he returned from his break with an impressive display in a maiden at Tramore in April. Setting a tempo which few of his rivals could live with and jumping fluently, Life In The Park was shaken up between the final two flights and came home 17 lengths clear of Butty O Brien.

The Tramore race was for conditional jockeys and winning rider Mikey O'Connor was on board again when Life In The Park followed up in the handicap hurdle for conditionals at the Punchestown Festival. He knuckled down to good effect to regain the lead in that contest, taking it up on the home turn before being headed by the eventual third Thanksforthehelp approaching the last. But the new leader wasn't helped by an awkward jump there and Life In The Park rallied on the run-in to beat the staying-on Rock Road by a length and three-quarters.

Life In The Park's half-brother Lifetime Ambition made into a smart novice chaser for Jessica Harrington in the latest season and also ran a good race at the Punchestown Festival, finishing second in the Champion Novice Chase over three miles in which Life In The Park's stablemate Bob Olinger disappointed. Life In The Park will be well suited by that trip himself, having only raced at around two and a half miles since making his Rules debut over slightly further. He would also have won his only start in points but fell at the last when clear. **Henry De Bromhead**

Conclusion: *Impressive winner of a maiden hurdle on his third start before following up in a conditionals' handicap at the Punchestown Festival and shapes like a staying chaser of the future for his Gold Cup-winning connections; will stay further than 21f*

Marine Nationale (Ire)   b111
5 b.g. French Navy – Power of Future (Ger) (Definite Article)
2021/22 NR :: 2022/23 b16.2g* b16.5g* Aug 20

It's nine years since owner Barry Connell's The Tullow Tank burst onto the scene. After graduating from bumpers, he had the world at his hooves at the start of the 2013/14 season, with victories in the Royal Bond Novice Hurdle and Future Champions Novice Hurdle giving him a Grade 1 double early in his career. Things didn't really work out for The Tullow Tank after that, however, and he was winless for his final trainer, Alan Fleming, who was the last man entrusted with Connell's horses before he decided to have a go at the training gig himself.

After saddling nine winners in Ireland in his first season with a licence, Connell was up to 12 in the last campaign and this season he's already off the mark, including with Marine Nationale, who made an impressive winning debut in a Punchestown bumper in May before defying a penalty to follow up in a similar event at Killarney in August. Given that the other previous winner in the line-up, Follow The Brave, finished lame at Killarney, Marine Nationale essentially had only one meaningful rival to beat, namely My Gaffer who had previously filled the runner-up spot in a Roscommon bumper. This race was all about one horse, though, as Marine Nationale dismissed the rest in the style of a smart prospect, leading on the bridle inside the final three furlongs and cruising clear from there to land the spoils by 11 lengths.

Marine Nationale is reported to have done plenty of jumping at home already and Connell has laid out a plan for him to take in the Royal Bond, a race won so dramatically by the aforementioned The Tullow Tank nine years ago. It's not an unrealistic target to go for, particularly as the A-listers from the Mullins yard aren't normally ready by late-November. With Marine Nationale already up and running, the Grade 1 dream is very much alive for Connell. **Barry Connell**

Conclusion: *Unbeaten in two starts in bumpers and has the makings of a smart novice hurdler*

SECTION

TALKING TO THE TRAINERS

We asked a number of leading National Hunt trainers to pick out a chaser, hurdler and novice to follow for the coming season. Here's what they said…

Harry Fry

Wins-Runs in Britain in 2021/22	**38/213**
Highest-rated horse in training	**Metier** Timeform Rating h143

Chaser: Revels Hill (c136): "He was progressive as a novice over fences, including when winning his last two starts at Taunton. He appeared to relish the step up in trip to three and a half miles and, although he will have to improve again, we hope he can be competitive in some of the bigger staying handicap chases this season."

Hurdler: Might I (h142): "He only won once as a novice but finished behind Constitution Hill and then Jonbon before placing in the Mersey Novices' Hurdle at Aintree in the spring. He's a half-brother to Stattler and we are looking forward to stepping him up in trip, with the valuable three-mile handicap hurdle at Haydock on Betfair Chase day a possible early-season target."

Novice: Dubrovnik Harry (h126): "He got off the mark over hurdles when winning easily at Exeter on New Year's Day. He rounded of the season with a very pleasing third-place effort in the EBF Final at Sandown. He has always looked a chaser and the plan is to go straight over fences off his hurdle rating."

Tom George

Wins-Runs in Britain in 2021/22	**33/262**
Highest-rated horse in training	**Come On Teddy** Timeform Rating c135

Chaser: Java Point (c133): "He won three chases last season and I would say he is still progressing. He should feature in a couple of big staying handicap chases."

Hurdler: Il Est Francais (h130p): "He's a four-year-old who won at Auteuil in March. He'll be seeing more of France than he will England and his first few runs will be over there."

Novice: What A Steal (b95): "He was placed in a couple of bumpers last season and I think the form has worked out quite well. He's a horse who should keep progressing in novice hurdles."

Nicky Henderson

Wins-Runs in Britain in 2021/22	**120/561**
Highest-rated horse in training	**Shishkin** Timeform Rating c181

Chaser: Mister Coffey (c138): "He ran a good race when second in the Kim Muir at Cheltenham. He's still a novice and he's got plenty of experience, so he can do lots of things."

Hurdler: Constitution Hill (h177p): "It's all fingers crossed that he's as good as what he showed us last season. He'll either start in the Fighting Fifth or the Ascot Hurdle, that's as far as we've got. We'll probably take him to the Christmas Hurdle and then we'll work out how we do it from there. It's the usual route and there isn't really a lot of variation to it. Then obviously the plan will be March and I suppose everybody would like to see the match with Honeysuckle."

Novice: Jonbon (h153p): "The plan is to go novice chasing with him and he's certainly going to stay further if needed. I suspect he'll start over two miles, but he could easily be going up to two and a half miles. He hasn't seen a fence in anger yet because the ground has been too firm and it's too early, but he's in good shape.

Philip Hobbs

Wins-Runs in Britain in 2021/22	**70/506**
Highest-rated horse in training	**Thyme Hill** Timeform Rating h158

Chaser: Celebre d'Allen (c142): "He won three of his four chases last season and has climbed from a BHA mark of 120 to 140, but we hope there could be further improvement."

Hurdler: Camprond (h145): "He improved all through last season and won well at the Punchestown Festival. He could improve again."

Novice: Mombasa (h135p): "He won his only two hurdles in France and has plenty of experience and ability for juvenile hurdles."

Emma Lavelle

Wins-Runs in Britain in 2021/22	**42/259**
Highest-rated horse in training	**Paisley Park** Timeform Rating h158

Chaser: Wouldubewell (c130): "She's a soft-ground mare who stays well. She had a really good season last season and finished with a confidence-boosting win at Bangor. She's got to keep going up but, the way that she races and how well she jumps, she could finish up being a Welsh National kind of horse if she can win one early doors when we get some soft ground."

Hurdler: **Nollyador (b104)**: "He ran some cracking races in bumpers last season and is a natural over an obstacle in his schooling. He could be a nice horse to look out for going hurdling."

Novice: **Young Butler (h121)**: "He won a couple over hurdles last season and is going to go over fences this term. He's a half-brother to Put The Kettle On and by Yeats, so he's a bit more of a stayer. I think Yeats' progeny tend to be slower to mature, but he's just blossomed so much through the summer and is definitely getting there now. I think he's a nice horse."

Donald McCain

Wins-Runs in Britain in 2021/22	**155/163**
Highest-rated horse in training	**Minella Drama** Timeform Rating c148

Chaser: **Tim Pat (c123p)**: "I was quite impressed with him at Haydock and I think there could be more to come. I know it wasn't a strong renewal of the Tim Molony and that isn't the race it used to be, but it was only his second run over fences and it was three and a half miles. He turned in absolutely running away, so that was a nice performance."

Hurdler: **Jungle Jack (h131)**: "Truthfully, I'm not 100% sure whether he'll go chasing or stay over hurdles. I don't think he's badly handicapped to stay hurdling if we feel we need to get a bit more experience into him, because he is a bit of a playboy. They're all bought to jump fences, but it's just a question of whether we do it straight away or not. If we go handicap hurdling and he goes and does very well in the short-term, then we might just wait a little bit longer. He could have run in the EBF Final where he was well-handicapped, but we thought we'd go a bit quieter because he is immature. We went to Bangor and, unfortunately, I think we met Alan King doing the same thing [with Harbour Lake]. I think they're two quite smart horses."

Novice: **Richmond Lake (h132)**: "The plan is to go over fences and he was a useful novice hurdler last season. Brian [Hughes, jockey] said he wasn't done with at Kelso when he came down and he probably didn't quite get over his fall there. He ran in points and looks every inch a chaser."

Olly Murphy

Wins-Runs in Britain in 2021/22   **92/527**

Highest-rated horse in training   **Brewin'Upastorm** Timeform Rating h153

Chaser: Gunsight Ridge (c133): "He had a couple of hard races mid-season and was favourite for the Red Rum at Aintree where he ran very flat. He could be a horse who could win a very good handicap this season."

Hurdler: Go Dante (h127): "He suffered an injury in the middle of last season, but he's always shown a lot at home. He could have a very nice handicap mark and hopefully he's a horse who can carry on progressing. It would be nice to think he could turn into a graded performer at some point."

Novice: Butch (b97): "He ran very well in a bumper at Huntingdon. He's got a very good pedigree, jumps well and could be a horse who can play in those bigger novice hurdles this season."

Paul Nicholls

Wins-Runs in Britain in 2021/22   **143/629**

Highest-rated horse in training   **Clan des Obeaux** Timeform Rating c168

Chaser: Greaneteen (c166): "He is a chaser to follow because I think the best is still to come from him. I think his best run was his last run in the Celebration Chase at Sandown in April. He loves Sandown and I think he could still be improving."

Hurdler: Henri The Second (b107+): "He won two bumpers last season and got struck into at Aintree, so you can put a line through that run. He's not unlike Stage Star, he's a big, scopey, chasing type of horse. We'll start him off in a maiden hurdle at somewhere like Chepstow and work up. Hopefully, he might be good enough to run in something like the Challow."

Novice: Monmiral (h147): "He's a smart horse and had a good record as a juvenile. We minded him a bit last season. He got an injury first time when he was struck into at Newcastle and then ran well in his two subsequent runs. By not doing too much with him, we've got a ready-made novice chaser for this season."

Fergal O'Brien

Wins-Runs in Britain in 2021/22   **128/739**

Highest-rated horse in training   **Paint The Dream** Timeform Rating c156

Chaser: **Imperial Alcazar (c154):** "He did great for us last season and I think there's a really big handicap in him somewhere. We're looking forward to getting going with him."

Hurdler: **Alaphilipe (h143):** "We're going to keep him over hurdles and try to get him qualified for the Pertemps Final again. Like Imperial Alcazar, he was second at Cheltenham last season."

Novice: **Manothepeople (h114):** "He won a couple over hurdles last season and is a very honest horse. He should make up into a lovely novice chaser over three miles plus."

Jonjo O'Neill

Wins-Runs in Britain in 2021/22   **82/507**

Highest-rated horse in training   **Soaring Glory** Timeform Rating h148

Chaser: **Garry Clermont (c131p):** "He goes novice chasing again this season after running in a few big handicap hurdles last term. He should be more mature this time round and is one we're looking forward to."

Hurdler: **Collectors Item (b103):** "He was just beaten by the Aintree Grade 2 bumper winner in a point and then ran a nice race at Newbury in a bumper. He is making good strides at home and will be one to look out for in novice hurdles."

Novice: **Are U Wise To That (b106):** "He won his bumper nicely at Warwick after he'd also finished second in a point. He is related to Denman and should be an improver in novice hurdles."

Ben Pauling

Wins-Runs in Britain in 2021/22   **44/341**

Highest-rated horse in training   **Global Citizen** Timeform Rating c147

Chaser: **Shakem Up'Arry (c135):** "The move to the new yard has transformed certain horses who had just struggled to hit the same sort of form regularly. He's a horse who has been quite hard to get spot on, but I think he's a huge talent on soft ground. I think he will genuinely stay two and a half miles and he'll go for the Paddy Power Gold Cup first-time-out. He's very good fresh and could be a horse to move through the chasing ranks nicely."

Hurdler: Severance (h128): "He hit the crossbar so many times last season and some might argue that the handicapper has him in his grasp, but I would strongly argue that he doesn't. He's just a horse who needs to find his stride and get his head back in front, then I think he can go on. He could be a Betfair Hurdle horse or something like that. He's a nice type, has a good attitude and is in good order."

Novice: Joe Dadancer (unraced): "He was bought privately in Ireland. He overjumped and fell at the last in his point when he was going far too well. He took off outside the wings and just didn't get his landing gear out. The time of that race was good and he's a gorgeous, big, strong horse. I'd be very surprised if he's not close to being one of the best novice hurdlers we've had."

David Pipe

Wins-Runs in Britain in 2021/22	**47/433**
Highest-rated horse in training	**Adagio** Timeform Rating h153

Chaser: Gericault Roque (c141p): "He is still only a six-year-old and open to further improvement over staying trips. He enjoyed an excellent first season over fences, culminating in a close second at the Cheltenham Festival in March. He remains a novice for the season ahead."

Hurdler: Oceanline (h113): "He won at Worcester in July on his first start for the stable where he beat a good yardstick on his first try at two and a half miles. He is still a novice over hurdles and could mix novice contests with handicaps. He should continue to pay his way."

Novice: Colony Queen (f97): "She was a most progressive mare on the Flat where she showed a great attitude to win 10 races. She seems to hurdle nicely at home and looks a nice prospect. She will be out in the autumn."

Lucinda Russell

Wins-Runs in Britain in 2021/22	**46/405**
Highest-rated horse in training	**Ahoy Senor** Timeform Rating c161p

Chaser: Ahoy Senor (c161p): "He's come out of the summer really well and we were delighted with him last season. It was a work in progress because he was a novice with his jumping, but I think by the end of the season he'd really sorted it out and I'm hoping he can build on that and improve. If he does, we could have a very exciting horse on our hands. He's obviously better around the flatter tracks, but I'm not scared to go back to Cheltenham and I'm hoping he'll run very well there in the spring. He'll be aimed at the Gold Cup, but I'm not quite sure yet where he'll start off this season."

Hurdler: **Our Marty (b90)**: "We had him as a two-year-old store and ran him in the juvenile bumpers last season. He didn't win but is a horse who is definitely going to improve over hurdles. He's one for novice hurdles this season."

Novice: **Haute Estime (h126)**: "She is a chaser and has always wanted to be a chaser. A late-maturing horse, she won a listed race over hurdles last season and was also third in the Sefton Novices' Hurdle at Aintree. That was a fantastic run against the boys and she is definitely a long-distance horse. She jumps really well and is a very bold mare, so she'll go chasing and is definitely one on my list."

Dan Skelton

Wins-Runs in Britain in 2021/22	**134/742**
Highest-rated horse in training	**Protektorat** Timeform Rating c164

Chaser: **Shan Blue (c159)**: "He started last season looking like he was going to win the Charlie Hall quite easily, but he fell and that put his whole season back. We then took our time getting him back and he did get somewhere near his best when he was second in a good handicap at Aintree. However, I think there is significantly more to come and we hope to see that this season."

Hurdler: **Get A Tonic (h131)**: "She took a big step up the ranks as a novice last season and learnt a lot when she was beaten by Marie's Rock in an open mares' hurdle at Warwick. I think she can go in all the mares' hurdles this season and I think she could be very progressive."

Novice: **Great Samourai (unraced)**: "We picked him up at the Goffs Sale in May. He is a son of Great Pretender with loads of scope and will definitely make a chaser in time. But he should make his mark in novice hurdles this season and is a very nice horse."

Joe Tizzard

Wins-Runs in Britain in 2021/22	**62/450**
Highest-rated horse in training	**Eldorado Allen** Timeform Rating c163

Chaser: **Oscar Elite (c141)**: "He's still a novice but was third in the Ultima at Cheltenham last season. He was pulled up at Aintree, but we found a little problem with his wind which we've tweaked. He's been second and third at two Cheltenham Festivals and I think there's a big pot in him."

Hurdler: **Bourbali (h124)**: "He won four last season and just progressed and progressed. He has a lovely attitude on him, a real forward-going horse. We'll aim him at the Silver Trophy at Chepstow and I think he could just progress again. He's a real nice chap."

Novice: **JPR One (h125)**: "He'll go novice chasing and I hold him in seriously high regard. I don't think he trained on in the second half of last season, but we've schooled him over fences and he's jumped like a buck. He just catches my eye every day of the week and he's a beautiful horse."

Evan Williams

Wins-Runs in Britain in 2021/22	**53/449**
Highest-rated horse in training	**Coole Cody** Timeform Rating c150

Chaser: **The Last Day (c142)**: "He might have a bit more to come if he gets a bit of luck. The handicapper didn't miss him last time, but he's still low mileage. He's old and he's got to improve, but you don't know where you can end up with those two-mile chasers. He could just make the breakthrough into graded company. He would have to improve, but you never know. He's never had his luck in life, he's always had a setback at the wrong time."

Hurdler: **Current Mood (h123)**: "She could be alright off her mark. She's done plenty of running, but she hasn't done much running in handicap company. She might be one for the Welsh Champion Hurdle if she got into it or one of those early-season races like the Silver Trophy. I was looking for a bit of black type all the time last season and she'd probably just gone over the top by her final start, but she could have a bit of movement in her mark."

Novice: **L'Astroboy (b104)**: "He won a bumper at Ffos Las and anything that wins a bumper for us has got to have some sort of ability. He's got a good way about him and is more of a chaser than a hurdler, but the fact he won a bumper is always a plus going into novice hurdles."

RISING STARS

Richard Bandey

Base	**Plantation Farm, Wolverton, Hampshire**
First Full Licence	**2018**
First Jumps Winner	**Alskamatic** Exeter 15/04/2014
Total Winners	**31**
Best Horse Trained	**Mister Malarky** Timeform Rating c152

Richard Bandey enjoyed much his best season in 2021/22 with a total of 19 winners from an increased string. Starting his training career in points, Bandey registered his first win under Rules in a novices' hunters' chase at Exeter in 2014 with Alskamatic, while his first winner after being granted a full licence in the autumn of 2018 came when Hard Station landed a gamble under Harry Bannister in a handicap chase at Market Rasen in November of that year. Winners proved few and far between for the next few years but all that changed last season, particularly from February onwards, with Bannister again in the saddle for all bar two of the stable's winners in 2021/22. New recruits to the yard contributed significantly to that success, none more so than Give Me A Moment, who was much improved over fences after being bought for just 8,000 guineas out of his Irish stable, with his win in a novices' handicap at Market Rasen in April being his fourth success from his last five starts. He hasn't stopped there, either, as he has since won twice more over hurdles this summer. The ex-French Saint Palais did really well, too, completing a hat-trick over fences in the Mandarin Handicap Chase at Bandey's local track, Newbury, in December when still only a four-year-old and later putting up a smart effort to win a good novices' handicap at Uttoxeter on the Midlands National card. He could reportedly go back over hurdles where he still has novice status. Another French recruit was cross-country chaser Diesel d'Allier, who already had winning form over Cheltenham's cross-country course for Emmanuel Clayeux. He soon proved better than ever for his new stable, winning a handicap over the same course in December and then being far from discredited when finishing fourth behind Delta Work and Tiger Roll at the Cheltenham Festival. The quality of the string was also boosted over the winter by the arrival of the smart but lazy staying chaser Mister Malarky, who'd seemed to have lost his way completely for Colin Tizzard. However, second places in the Grimthorpe at Doncaster and at Cheltenham's April meeting on his two starts for Bandey in the spring showed he'd benefited from the change of scenery.

Gary Hanmer

Base	**Church Farm, Tattenhall, Cheshire**
First Full Licence	**2015**
First Jumps Winner	**Mountain Cabin** Bangor 15/05/1993
Total Winners	**87**
Best Horse Trained	**Wbee** Timeform Rating h134

Not all Rising Stars are necessarily overnight successes and that's certainly true in Gary Hanmer's case. His first winner under Rules came nearly 30 years ago, though the result of the North Western Area Point To Point Championship Final Hunters' Chase at Bangor could have been even better for Hanmer as he had two runners in the race but partnered the shorter-priced of the pair instead of the 16/1 winner Mountain Cabin. But over 25 years there were plenty of successes in both a riding and training capacity for Hanmer on the point-to-point circuit with the occasional hunter chase victory as well. In 2015, Hanmer took out a full training licence which resulted in more success, although his seasonal tallies initially remained in single figures. But there was a step-change in the yard's fortunes last season which resulted in 32 wins at a strike rate of 22% which made Hanmer a very profitable trainer to follow as a profit of £75.29 to a £1 stake would have been made backing the stable's runners. It was notable that several of them managed to stay ahead of the handicapper during the season, with the likes of Isthebaropen and Steel Wave winning three times, Wbee and Hillview four times and fairly useful two-mile chaser Sir Tivo winning six races. Wbee enjoyed an unbeaten campaign which he capped with a win in a three-mile handicap hurdle at Cheltenham's April meeting worth £10,000. More than half of the stable's winners last season came in the period May to September and they've been similarly productive this summer with 16 winners on the board by the end of August. Most of the horses named above have already won again this season. Wbee won an £18,000 contest at Cartmel in May for the second year running, the fact that he gained his latest win off a mark 18 lb higher than the year before showing how much improvement he has made in the interim. Cartmel is one of the tracks where Hanmer has had the most success in recent seasons behind only local course Bangor, Stratford and Southwell.

Kieran Callaghan

Attached Stable	**Willie Mullins**
First Ride	**2020**
First Winner	**Jumping Jet** Gowran Park 02/03/2021
Total Winners	**7**
Best Jumps Horses Ridden	**Ganapathi** Timeform Rating c141

It's worth taking note if a rider with as much as experience as Patrick Mullins describes a teenager as 'a jockey with a big future'. Mullins was speaking after Kieran Callaghan's biggest win to date, and his first over fences, which came on Rock Road, trained by his father Willie, in the Mayo National at Ballinrobe in May. Mullins senior also paid Callaghan a big compliment when nominating him to replace stable jockey Paul Townend, who'd been stood down after sustaining an injury the day before, on Stratum in a race at Cork in August. However, the stewards intervened, ruling that substituting Townend with a 7-lb claimer wasn't a like-for-like replacement and Stratum had to be withdrawn. Mullins disagreed with their decision, explaining 'Paul was injured and I felt Kieran was an adequate replacement. He's ridden winners for me and I was very happy to give him an opportunity on a top-class horse.' There should be plenty more such opportunities for Callaghan in future. He has ridden five of his seven winners to date for Mullins having had his first ride for Closutton when third in a bumper at the 2021 Galway Festival. Callaghan's most recent win for Mullins came in a beginners chase at Clonmel in June on Bacardys, who finally opened his account over fences at the age of 11. That was a feather in the cap for Callaghan on a horse who's prone to mistakes over fences and had hit the deck with both Townend and Ruby Walsh in the saddle earlier in his chasing career, though Callaghan himself met the same fate two starts later. Callaghan was only 17 when riding his first winner on just his second ride the previous spring. That came on Jumping Jet for trainer Barry Fitzgerald in a mares' bumper at Gowran Park.

Mark McDonagh

Attached Stable	**Michael Hourigan, Aengus King**
First Ride	**2017**
First Winner	**Blackjack Boy** Listowel 21/09/2020
Total Winners	**30**
Best Jumps Horses Ridden	**Roi Mage** Timeform Rating c143x

Riding a Cheltenham Festival winner must be the dream of every conditional jockey and for 20-year-old Mark McDonagh, who was still combining race riding with studying for a business degree at the time, that dream came true on what was not just his very first ride at the Festival, but also his first ride in Britain, when winning the Martin Pipe Conditional Jockeys' Handicap Hurdle on the Joseph O'Brien-trained Banbridge. The next day, McDonagh finished second on Young Dev in the Midlands Grand National at Uttoxeter but went one better in another 'National' just 24 hours later when Spades Are Trumps ran out an easy winner of the Ulster version at Downpatrick for Gavin Cromwell in the colours of J. P. McManus. McDonagh, who says Paul Carberry was his favourite jockey growing up, started riding out for his grandfather Michael and also did a lot of showjumping ('until I was 16 and wanted to go a bit quicker') before riding briefly as an amateur. But it was soon after turning conditional that he rode his first two winners, Blackjack Boy and Drumcoo, at the Listowel Festival in September 2020 for Eric McNamara and Michael Hourigan respectively. Another landmark in McDonagh's early career was riding his first double, which came at Tramore the following autumn, and one of those Tramore winners, Nell's Well, pulled off a 25/1 win when giving McDonagh a Grade 3 success in a novice hurdle at Cork last December when he was unable to claim his 7 lb. Prior to his Cheltenham Festival win, McDonagh was also successful at the Dublin Racing Festival when winning the Leopardstown Handicap Chase on another McManus horse, Birchdale, for Enda Bolger. McDonagh rode 15 winners in all in Ireland last season and looks well on the way to beating that total with nine winners on the board already in the current campaign. However, first he'll have to complete his recovery from breaking three ribs in a fall at Downpatrick in July, having already bounced back from a broken shoulder blade which kept him out of the Punchestown Festival.

ANTE-POST BETTING

Timeform's John Ingles takes a look at the markets for some of the highlights in the National Hunt calendar and picks out his best value bets…

Queen Mother Champion Chase winner Energumene was the success story from this preview last year, selected at 5/1 and going on to give Willie Mullins an overdue first success in the race at an SP of 5/2. It could be argued that luck was on our side on that occasion, given that chief rival Shishkin was plainly amiss, but there was the usual quota of ante-post woe to balance things out. Gold Cup hope Monkfish produced a sick note for the whole season almost before the ink was dry on his name, Galopin des Champs excelled but, unfortunately for us, as a novice chaser rather than as a Stayers' Hurdle candidate, while a tornado blew away Clan des Obeaux's bid to win a third King George…

King George VI Chase

The King George had its longest priced winner in the race's history when 28/1 chance **Tornado Flyer** beat our selection, the former dual winner **Clan des Obeaux**, into second last season under unusually testing conditions for the race. Given the winner's efforts since, it would be no less surprising if he can stage a repeat this season, but Willie Mullins could easily win the race for the second year running if **Allaho** takes his chance. He routed a field of established stayers–the previous year's winner Clan des Obeaux was runner-up and Tornado Flyer was well beaten–in the Punchestown Gold Cup in April when reproducing his top-notch form over shorter trips for a first win over three miles over fences. Kempton looks an ideal track, too, for Allaho's bold-jumping, catch-me-if-you-can style of racing. However, Paul Nicholls has a potentially stronger candidate than Clan des Obeaux this time in **Bravemansgame** whose four wins last term included the Kauto Star Novices' Chase on the King George card when beating **Ahoy Senor**. But it's Lucinda Russell's runner-up who makes more appeal at longer odds. A big, raw-boned gelding, he was much less the finished article than the winner at Kempton last Christmas and the pace he set on that occasion didn't bring out the best in him either. Having beaten the subsequent Grand National winner Noble Yeats at Wetherby, Ahoy Senor ended his season with a convincing win in the Mildmay Novices' Chase at Aintree, turning the tables not only on Bravemansgame but also **L'Homme Presse** who'd beaten him at Cheltenham. Ahoy Senor tends to jump slightly to his right, so going that way round at Kempton will be in his favour, and he appeals as a longer-priced each-way alternative to favourite Allaho.

SELECTION: Ahoy Senor (16/1) each-way

Champion Hurdle

Honeysuckle has a third Champion Hurdle in her sights next March in what will be her final season of racing. But whether or not she emulates Istabraq and the four earlier triple Champion Hurdle winners, Honeysuckle is assured of a special place in jump racing history thanks to an unbeaten record that currently stretches to 16 starts after she won the Punchestown Champion Hurdle again. It's taking nothing away from Honeysuckle's record to point out the weakness of the two-mile hurdling division, particularly in Britain, a situation her mares' allowance has enabled her to exploit to the full. At least, that has been the case so far. But Willie Mullins has as many as three new potential challengers in **State Man**, **Vauban** and **Sir Gerhard**, Cheltenham Festival winners in the County Hurdle, Triumph Hurdle and Ballymore Novices' Hurdle respectively. Of those, State Man appeals most having gone on to win a Grade 1 novice at Punchestown, while Sir Gerhard, who was beaten at Punchestown, looks more of a chaser to us. But all three still need to improve to challenge Honeysuckle whereas Britain's top novice, **Constitution Hill**, already has form in the book which

All roads lead to the Champion Hurdle for Constitution Hill

isn't far behind the sort of ratings Istabraq produced. That seems remarkable for a novice who's had just the three starts for Nicky Henderson, but it was a breathtaking performance from Constitution Hill to inflict the only defeat so far in the career of smart stablemate Jonbon by 22 lengths in the Supreme Novices' Hurdle in a time over five seconds faster than Honeysuckle's Champion Hurdle. Constitution Hill is no bigger than 7/4 for the Champion Hurdle at the time of writing, but with little to fear from would-be rivals in Britain before then, there's a good chance he'll be a fair bit shorter still by next March.

SELECTION: Constitution Hill (7/4)

Queen Mother Champion Chase

Last year, it was **Energumene** who looked the value for the Queen Mother Champion Chase compared to **Shishkin** but, with even less on Timeform ratings between the two best chasers in training, the same reasoning means we'll be jumping ship to Nicky Henderson's chaser who's around twice the price of his rival this time. Energumene might be the safer bet, admittedly, having followed up his Cheltenham win with a top-notch display against his stable's former top two-miler Chacun Pour Soi at Punchestown. Shishkin, on the other hand, was last seen pulling up behind Energumene at Cheltenham, but it's highly encouraging that his trainer reports that he has now fully recovered from the rare bone condition which accounted for that odds-on defeat which ended his campaign. The Champion Chase was no race to judge Shishkin on but go back a couple of months earlier and it was he who came out on top in a much fairer fight with Energumene in the Clarence House Chase at Ascot which was one of the races of the season. Shishkin, who has won all his completed starts, wouldn't be the first Champion Chase winner from his stable, either, to overcome a setback along the way, both Sprinter Sacre and Altior having done so successfully. Energumene and Shishkin set a very high standard which will be hard for the best novices from last season to reach. Arkle winner **Edwardstone** is thoroughly likeable but wasn't an outstanding winner of that race and his unexposed Aintree conqueror **Gentleman de Mee** has the more scope to improve. Another of Energumene's stablemates **Ferny Hollow** clearly has lots of talent, too, but he hasn't made it as far as the New Year in his last two campaigns and single-figure odds about him aren't that tempting given his apparent fragility.

SELECTION: Shishkin (4/1)

Stayers' Hurdle

Flooring Porter is ante-post favourite to win his third Stayers' Hurdle and if successful that would put him alongside Inglis Drever and Big Buck's, the only others to have won the race more than twice. But while Flooring Porter has been a gutsy winner of the Stayers' Hurdle after making all the running at the last two Festivals, there's little on form between several of the leading staying hurdlers. **Klassical Dream** looks better value at twice the favourite's odds. He had excuses when only fifth in the Stayers' Hurdle but beat Flooring Porter for the second time when winning the Christmas Hurdle at Leopardstown and after Cheltenham won his second Champion Stayers' Hurdle at Punchestown before finishing a good second in the Grande Course de Haies d'Auteuil. **The Nice Guy**, who won the Grade 1 staying novice hurdles at both Cheltenham and Punchestown and is still unbeaten, seems set to go chasing instead, while **Buzz**, another prominent in the betting, fractured his pelvis after winning the Coral Hurdle at Ascot last November and isn't yet proven beyond two and a half miles. **Thyme Hill** was second to Flooring Porter at Cheltenham only to run a lacklustre race at Aintree next time and, in an open division, it could therefore be worth taking a chance on another from the Philip Hobbs stable. **Sporting John**'s form in handicaps last season would have put him in the mix in the top staying hurdles. As well as winning a listed event at Cheltenham under 11-12 in November, he won a Pertemps Qualifier at Warwick in January but wasn't seen out again. However, the third from that race, Third Wind, went on to win the Pertemps Final, while the fourth, Sire du Berlais,

Sporting John (right) could develop into a key contender for the Stayers' Hurdle

a former Stayers' Hurdle runner-up, had Flooring Porter and Thyme Hill behind him when winning the Liverpool Hurdle at Aintree.

SELECTION: **Sporting John (33/1)**

Cheltenham Gold Cup

A Plus Tard has never finished out of the first three, including at the last four Cheltenham Festivals, and as he'll still be only nine next March, he seems sure to mount a solid defence of his Gold Cup title. But most lists have him second favourite behind last season's outstanding novice **Galopin des Champs**, who would be unbeaten over fences but for his last-fence fall in the Turners Novices' Chase. His jumping isn't a concern on the whole but, having been campaigned at around two and a half miles over fences so far, it begs the question of whether or not he'll even contest the Gold Cup. However, Galopin des Champs' only try to date over three miles was a successful one in a Grade 1 novice hurdle at Punchestown and Willie Mullins has **Allaho** for the Ryanair Chase. In the same ownership as A Plus Tard, a hat-trick bid by Allaho in the Ryanair seems most likely, but current odds of 10/1 would look big if for some reason he went for the Gold Cup instead, especially now that he's won the Punchestown Gold Cup. **Monkfish** was our Gold Cup selection last year, just weeks before a tendon injury ruled him out for the season, so we'll be wishing him well but hoping he's not jumping the last upsides this year's pick **L'Homme Presse**, who succeeded him on the

L'Homme Presse should relish the Gold Cup trip

Brown Advisory Novices' Chase roll of honour. That was a second win of the season at Cheltenham for Venetia Williams' highly progressive novice, who was very strong at the finish, suggesting he'll relish the Gold Cup trip. His jumping was much better than that of runner-up **Ahoy Senor**, who took his revenge in their rematch at Aintree, but L'Homme Presse can be forgiven that first defeat over fences and looks worth an each-way interest.

SELECTION: **L'Homme Presse (14/1) each way**

Grand National

It turned out that the Grand National winner had never even raced over fences when this preview was written last year and, even on the day, 50/1 shot **Noble Yeats**, a novice who'd been beaten an aggregate of more than 60 lengths in three previous handicaps over fences, was scarcely any easier to find. On the plus side, he had Sam Waley-Cohen in the saddle, but Noble Yeats won't have the assistance of the amateur with a superb record over the National fences in any future attempts as he announced his retirement after the race. Noble Yeats and runner-up **Any Second Now**, who'd been third the year before, head the ante-post betting for next year's race but, in the hope that the 2023 winner does at least have some chasing experience already, we'll pick a couple at long odds to maintain recent Irish success in the race. **Ontheropes** was one of Willie Mullins' National entries last year but wasn't seen out after staying on for fifth in the Thyestes Handicap Chase at Gowran in January when shaping as though worth a try over a marathon trip. He'd won the three-mile Munster National earlier in the season and his trainer has described him as 'a really good jumper' who 'wants nice ground', so he has the right sort of profile. So too does **Frontal Assault** for Gordon Elliott. He didn't win in his first season over fences but was crying out for a step up in distance and duly ran his best race on his final start when second in the Irish Grand National after making much of the running. Frontal Assault is unexposed as a staying chaser and should have won a race or two before hopefully going to Aintree.

SELECTIONS: **Ontheropes and Frontal Assault (both 50/1)**

LEADING JUMPS SIRES

King's Theatre was champion for the fifth and final time in 2016/17 but since then the title of leading jumps sire in Britain and Ireland has changed hands much more frequently. There was another new name at the top of the list last season when **Yeats** became champion. Best known as a racehorse for his four Gold Cup wins for Aidan O'Brien, Yeats stood for €5,000 at Coolmore's Castlehyde Stud in 2022, half the fee he stood for in his first season there in 2010.

Crucial to Yeats' title was the first prize of £500,000 won by Noble Yeats when successful in the Grand National, though he wasn't the best of his sire's jumpers last season. Irish Gold Cup winner Conflated was his highest-rated chaser, while Flooring Porter, who retained his Stayers' Hurdle title, was Yeats' best hurdler. Cotswold Chase winner Chantry House, Rehearsal Chase winner Aye Right and Thyestes Chase winner Longhouse Poet were other notable staying chasers who helped their sire to the title.

Runner-up in the table was **Fame And Glory**, himself an Ascot Gold Cup winner, and the only sire during the season to have more wins and individual winners than Yeats. Fame And Glory died in 2017 after siring just five crops, but he has left behind plenty of good horses, the eldest of whom are still only eight-year-olds, so he'll make an impact for a while yet. The young profile of his runners means that hurdlers dominate, with Coral Cup winner Commander of Fleet his highest-rated horse. Albert Bartlett Novices' Hurdle winner The Nice Guy gave Fame And Glory a second Cheltenham Festival winner, while Glory And Fortune became his second consecutive Betfair Hurdle winner after Soaring Glory.

Getaway was the third sire to be represented by more than 100 individual winners during the season. Given that he had more runners than any other sire, Getaway's notable winners were quite few and far between, with the likes of Sporting John, who won a listed handicap hurdle at Cheltenham and a Pertemps Qualifier at Warwick, and the Kerry National winner Assemble the best of them.

Kapgarde was the only French-based sire in the top 10 and, while that gave him fewer runners in Britain and Ireland than the other leading sires, they included no fewer than three top-class chasers. They were headed by A Plus Tard, who went one better than the year before to win the Cheltenham Gold Cup as well as another of Britain's biggest chasing prizes, the Betfair Chase. Clan des Obeaux had to settle for second in his bid to win the King George VI Chase for the third time, though he did win his second Bowl Chase at Aintree. Fakir d'Oudairies retained his Melling Chase title at the latter track and picked up another Grade 1 in Britain, the Ascot Chase.

Milan, the leading jumps sire in 2019/20, was fifth this time, the injury sustained by what remains his most exciting prospect My Drogo after just two starts over fences being a big blow to his earnings potential. That meant Marie's Rock, whose wins included the David Nicholson Mares' Hurdle at Cheltenham and the Mares Champion Hurdle at Punchestown, was Milan's highest earner of the season, just ahead of Santini, who didn't win but was runner-up in the Cotswold Chase and fourth in the Grand National.

Flemensfirth, who was champion in 2017/18 and 2018/19 but is now retired from stud duties, was next in the table. He's still capable of coming up with big winners as he showed when Tornado Flyer caused an upset in the King George VI Chase. Former stars Waiting Patiently and Magic of Light were both retired last season, but Flemensfirth still has promising types coming through, including Dusart, a smart novice chaser for Nicky Henderson last season, and the Albert Bartlett runner-up and Leopardstown Grade 1 novice hurdle winner Minella Cocooner.

Shirocco in seventh is the second son of Monsun in the table after Getaway. None of his current jumpers are in the same league as his Champion Hurdle winner Annie Power, but he did have another Festival winner when Third Wind won the Pertemps Final. Queens Brook went close in the Mares' Hurdle, while smart chaser Fortescue was Shirocco's biggest winner over fences in the listed Swinley Handicap Chase at Ascot.

Shantou died last September at the age of 28 having been retired from stud duties in 2020. As well as the season's most prolific winner, Minella Trump, winner of eight races for Donald McCain, his other chasers included the Troytown winner Run Wild Fred, and Death Duty and The Galloping Bear, who won the Grand National Trials at Punchestown and Haydock respectively.

Stowaway and **Jeremy**, who complete the top 10, have had posthumous success for several seasons now. Stowaway was the leading sire in 2020/21, but the absence of his best jumper Monkfish last season was a big setback to his chances of retaining his title. On the other hand, Stattler and Fury Road were among the best in the latest crop of staying novice chasers and Hillcrest could be another in that category this season. Jeremy's 2021 runaway Supreme Novices' Hurdle winner Appreciate It had to miss most of the season, but stablemate Sir Gerhard won the latest Ballymore Novices' Hurdle and Corach Rambler gave him another Festival winner in the Ultima Handicap Chase.

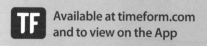

SECTION

TIMEFORM'S VIEW

Chosen from the Timeform formbook, here is Timeform's detailed analysis— compiled by our team of race reporters—of a selection of key races from Cheltenham.

CHELTENHAM Tuesday March 15
GOOD

Sky Bet Supreme Novices' Hurdle (Grade 1) (1)

Pos	Btn	Horse	Age	Wgt	Eq	Trainer	Jockey	SP
1		CONSTITUTION HILL	5	11-7		Nicky Henderson	Nico de Boinville	9/4jf
2	22	JONBON (FR)	6	11-7		Nicky Henderson	Aidan Coleman	5/1
3	2½	KILCRUIT (IRE)	7	11-7	(t)	W. P. Mullins, Ireland	Mr P. W. Mullins	6/1
4	8½	BRING ON THE NIGHT	5	11-7	(t)	W. P. Mullins, Ireland	B. J. Cooper	28/1
5	24	JPR ONE (IRE)	5	11-7		Colin Tizzard	Brendan Powell	150/1
F		DYSART DYNAMO (IRE)	6	11-7	(t)	W. P. Mullins, Ireland	P. Townend	9/4jf
F		SHALLWEHAVEONEMORE (FR)	5	11-7		Gary Moore	Joshua Moore	40/1
pu		MIGHTY POTTER (FR)	5	11-7		Gordon Elliott, Ireland	J. W. Kennedy	15/2
pu		SILENT REVOLUTION (IRE)	6	11-7		Paul Nicholls	Harry Cobden	125/1

9 ran Race Time 3m 45.20 Closing Sectional (4.10f): 55.20s (102.0%) Winning Owner: Mr Michael Buckley

With the Covid pandemic having been shifted from the headlines by a shockingly brutal war, an event recognised in the title of the NH Chase, something like normality returned to the Cheltenham Festival, though there was nothing normal about the performance of Constitution Hill, who produced a stunning effort that looks as good at this stage as any by a novice hurdler in Timeform's experience, his initial rating ahead of those given to both the ill-fated Golden Cygnet in this race in 1978 and Alderbrook in winning the 1995 Champion Hurdle as a novice, that view of the form backed up by both the time and the closing sectional, this race quicker at all stages than the much more steadily-run Champion Hurdle, this strongly run, with 2 high-quality novices giving the winner a lead, nothing else in the second successive single-figure field for this race ever involved, the winner's turn of foot off the final bend electric, his performance that of a future Champion Hurdle winner for sure; with a record first-day crowd after last season's ghostly staging behind closed doors, the Cheltenham roar returned, and so too did false starts, 3 on the afternoon, though the one here having less impact than the later ones, the riders here and in the Ultima found not to be in breach of the guidelines, though, due to Covid restrictions still in place in the weighing room, there wasn't a socially-distanced naughty step big enough for the riders who were involved in the Fred Winter false start and the matter was referred to the BHA headquarters. **Constitution Hill** produced what, on initial assessment, looks the best performance by a novice hurdler in Timeform's long experience, albeit in a strongly-run race set up for an exceptional horse to run to a very high figure, able to sit comfortably behind the gallop and finding a fine turn of foot away from the mud, strong at the finish too; tracked pace, travelled strongly, loomed up 2 out, led soon after, quickened clear, kept on well run-in, impressive; on paper this performance would have been good enough to have won the Champion Hurdle later on the card and he poses a very real threat to Honeysuckle, a meeting between the pair potentially happening as soon as Punchestown, it going almost without saying that he is the most exciting hurdling prospect for many a year. **Jonbon** lost his unbeaten record, though he emerged with plenty of credit against one out of the ordinary, their paths surely now likely to diverge, with the 2023 Arkle surely the long-term plan, everything about him suggesting a better chaser than even the smart horse he is over hurdles; close up, travelled well, led 3 out, shaken up soon after, headed soon after 2 out, no match for winner. **Kilcruit** runner-up in last season's Champion Bumper, ran creditably on his first attempt in graded company over hurdles, kept to 2m, though without ever really looking likely to get involved, his performance suggesting another try over further might be worth a go; waited with, mistake first, effort before 3 out, stayed on straight, never on terms; he has the physique to make a chaser. **Bring On The Night** the one ex-Flat performer in the field, lacked the experience needed to make any sort of impact in this, less than 3 weeks after his hurdling debut, in a tongue strap this time; in rear, not always fluent, shaken up before fifth, plugged on straight, never a threat; he isn't an imposing sort, certainly not judged against the pick of these jumping-breds, but he remains capable of better in calmer waters. **JPR One** had left the impression he wasn't ready for a test like the Betfair Hurdle last time and he certainly wasn't up to this demanding task, either in terms of ability or know-how, run off his feet; raced off the pace, not fluent third, labouring before 3 out, hampered there. **Dysart Dynamo** under less testing conditions, was strong in the betting and still just about in front when he came down, though he wouldn't have got anywhere near the winner and, given how far out it was, it's hard to say where he would have finished in relation to the runner-up; led, took keen hold, not fluent first, second, ridden when fell 3 out; a strong sort, who looked dull in his coat beforehand, he has the makings of a leading novice chaser next season. **Shallwehaveonemore** met a sad end; held up, off the bridle when hampered 3 out, fell fatally last. **Mighty Potter** was in a stronger Grade 1 than the one he'd won at Christmas and couldn't cope, even if it's likely that he'd have benefited from more testing conditions; waited with, hung right, not fluent fourth, blundered fifth, lost place soon after, pulled up before 2 out. **Silent Revolution** had a lot to find in this exalted company after just one run in a small-field novice and he lacked both the class and experience to cope after 4 months off; raced off the pace, labouring early final circuit, behind when blundered fifth, pulled up.

Sporting Life Arkle Challenge Trophy Novices' Chase (Grade 1) (1)

Pos	Btn	Horse	Age	Wgt	Eq	Trainer	Jockey	SP
1		EDWARDSTONE	8	11-4		Alan King	Tom Cannon	5/2f
2	4¼	GABYNAKO (FR)	7	11-4	(t)	Gavin Patrick Cromwell, Ireland	Keith Donoghue	25/1
3	3½	BLUE LORD (FR)	7	11-4	(t)	W. P. Mullins, Ireland	P. Townend	4/1
4	3	WAR LORD (GER)	7	11-4		Colin Tizzard	Brendan Powell	50/1
5	2	RIVIERE D'ETEL (FR)	5	10-11		Gordon Elliott, Ireland	J. W. Kennedy	7/2
6	3½	HAUT EN COULEURS (FR)	5	11-4		W. P. Mullins, Ireland	B. J. Cooper	6/1
7	12	COEUR SUBLIME (IRE)	7	11-4	(t)	Henry de Bromhead, Ireland	Rachael Blackmore	18/1
8	34	MAGIC DAZE (IRE)	6	10-11		Henry de Bromhead, Ireland	D. J. O'Keeffe	12/1
F		BRAVE SEASCA (FR)	7	11-4		Venetia Williams	Charlie Deutsch	80/1
F		RED ROOKIE	7	11-4		Emma Lavelle	Tom Bellamy	80/1
ur		SAINT SAM (FR)	5	11-4	(h)	W. P. Mullins, Ireland	S. F. O'Keeffe	12/1

11 ran Race Time 3m 52.60 Closing Sectional (3.75f): 53.9s (101.8%) Winning Owner: Robert Abrey & Ian Thurtle

An Arkle that lacked a potential star of the brightness of Shishkin, Altior or Sprinter Sacre, ones who could have potentially fitted that bill, My Drogo and Ferny Hollow, on the sidelines, another, Appreciate It, not seen out this season until an hour after this race, though the winner in an otherwise representative field was a thoroughly deserved one, the really likeable Edwardstone crowning a full campaign with a second win at Grade 1 level. **Edwardstone** is a thoroughly likeable sort, who took his winning sequence to 5 since brought down on his return, doing well early to avoid that fate again here, everything else going smoothly for him, clearly a high-class novice, though whether he has the ability to pose a threat to the very good established 2m chasers if they remain at their current level something of a doubt, solid and reliable as he is; handy, went with zest, hampered fourth, headway on bridle after 3 out, led when hampered 2 out, shaken up before last, kept on well, ridden out. **Gabynako** in first-time tongue strap, had been supplemented for this and rewarded connections admirably, running his best race, well served by coming from off a good gallop at this shorter trip; held up, travelled well, headway after 3 out, ridden next, stayed on run-in, no impression on winner. **Blue Lord** lost his unbeaten record over fences, his keenness something of an issue this time, more involved in the race than his rider probably desired; not fluent second, pulled way into prominent position fourth, shaken up home turn, not quicken run-in. **War Lord** had plenty on at this level and ran up to his best, rather like when he was runner-up to Edwardstone in the Henry VIII picking off a couple of tiring runners late on to make the frame; handy, shaken up 3 out, lost place soon after, stayed on again run-in; he's been kept to 2m over fences but had form over further over hurdles. **Riviere d'Etel** looked the main danger to the winner on form, but ran below her best, constantly adjusting right over these demanding fences and probably doing more than ideal at the head of affairs as well; prominent, jumped right, led before 3 out, headed when bumped 2 out, weakened run-in (lost shoe). **Haut En Couleurs** was a bit short on experience, but this was still a rather disappointing effort, in that he didn't see his race out and ran some way below the level of his chasing debut; held up, took keen hold, mistake second, effort 3 out, not fluent last 2, weakened run-in. **Coeur Sublime** was well held, making no impact back at Grade 1 level, away from soft ground; raced off the pace, labouring 3 out, mistake and hampered last. **Magic Daze** ran poorly after 3 months off, very much on her toes beforehand and doing far too much in front to last home; led, pulled hard, headed before 3 out, weakened soon after. **Brave Seasca** up against it at this level, didn't get very far anyway; disputed lead, fell fourth. **Red Rookie** on his toes beforehand, was very much up against it in this company and, though no threat at any stage, would have run at least as well as previously had he not come down at the last; raced off the pace, ridden 3 out, not quicken, fell last. **Saint Sam** failed to complete through no fault of his own; held up, mistake first, hampered and unseated fourth.

Unibet Champion Hurdle Challenge Trophy (Grade 1) (1)

Pos	Btn	Horse	Age	Wgt	Eq	Trainer	Jockey	SP
1		HONEYSUCKLE	8	11-3		Henry de Bromhead, Ireland	Rachael Blackmore	8/11f
2	3½	EPATANTE (FR)	8	11-3		Nicky Henderson	Aidan Coleman	16/1
3	1	ZANAHIYR (IRE)	5	11-10	(s+t)	Gordon Elliott, Ireland	J. W. Kennedy	28/1
4	2¾	SAINT ROI (FR)	7	11-10	(t)	W. P. Mullins, Ireland	M. P. Walsh	33/1
5	1½	GLORY AND FORTUNE (IRE)	7	11-10	(t)	Tom Lacey	Stan Sheppard	150/1
6	nk	NOT SO SLEEPY	10	11-10		Hughie Morrison	Jonathan Burke	125/1
7	nk	APPRECIATE IT (IRE)	8	11-10		W. P. Mullins, Ireland	P. Townend	10/3
8	5½	ADAGIO (GER)	5	11-10	(t)	David Pipe	Tom Scudamore	28/1
9	12	TOMMY'S OSCAR (IRE)	7	11-10		Ann Hamilton	Danny McMenamin	25/1
10	6	TEAHUPOO (FR)	5	11-10		Gordon Elliott, Ireland	Robbie Power	9/1

10 ran Race Time 3m 50.80 Closing Sectional (4.10f): 55.8s (103.4%) Winning Owner: Mr K. Alexander

Honeysuckle looked to have a lot in hand on form against rivals that had mostly shown themselves to have something to find to win an average Champion Hurdle, and she became the third odds-on winner of the race in the last decade, following Buveur d'Air, for his second win, and Faugheen, the lack of serious opposition shown up by her main market rival having been absent for a year, her victory almost routine, beating a pair that she'd defeated comfortably before, her form in a race run at an ordinary gallop probably not quite so good as that she showed when winning this in 2021, a much bigger threat to her hat-trick bid in 2023 having emerged at the start of the afternoon. **Honeysuckle** duly followed up her win in the 2021 Champion Hurdle, this her third Festival success in all, everything unfolding ideally for her (that she didn't trade above evens in running testament to the straightforwardness of her task), her turn of foot decisive into the straight, strong up the run-in as well, after a good jump looked necessary at the last, just to keep her in control; in touch, jumped fluently, travelled strongly, quickened to lead soon after 2 out, jumped left last, drew clear run-in, ridden out; she's a class apart from the established 2m hurdlers, though Constitution Hill is obviously a very potent threat to her dominance. **Epatante** was placed for the third time in 3 attempts in the Champion Hurdle, running as well as she did when winning in 2020, just beaten by a superior mare, though she'd have been perhaps a length closer without her mistake at the last; waited with, went with enthusiasm, effort 2 out, keeping on when mistake last, no impression on winner. **Zanahiyr** in first-time cheekpieces, ran at least as well as previously, though beaten fair and square, at least the headgear looking to have a positive impact, the Aintree Hurdle over further perhaps worth a try, as he gives the impression he will stay; handy, travelled well, every chance 2 out, not quicken home turn, not fluent last, kept on. **Saint Roi** in first-time tongue strap, finished fourth in a Grade 1 for the fourth time in his last 5 starts, running up to his best, though without posing much of a threat and very much a known quantity now, not the easiest to place; held up, headway when mistake 2 out, ridden after, stayed on run-in, never on terms. **Glory And Fortune** seemed to excel himself, back in Grade 1 company, though there was clearly an element of picking up the pieces, ridden quietly and passing the couple that had set the pace late on, no threat to the principals; held up, not fluent fourth, shaken up 3 out, stayed on approaching last, nearest at the finish. **Not So Sleepy** was better behaved than at Kempton and ran close to his best, essentially just not good enough in the very best company; chased leader, took keen hold, upsides third, shaken up before 3 out, outpaced next, plugged on run-in. **Appreciate It** a chaser on looks, hadn't been seen since a wide-margin winner of the 2021 Supreme and returning in this can't have been the plan, his jumping suggesting one schooled over fences, his appearance beforehand, a bit sweaty and with something to work on, mirrored by the way he didn't quite see out the race, enough in his effort to suggest his ability remains and a bolder showing potentially to come at Punchestown; led, not always fluent, travelled well, shaken up 2 out, headed soon after, no extra approaching last. **Adagio** has a good record at this track, but had plenty to find at this level and was below form in first-time tongue strap, unlikely to have got involved even before he clobbered one; held up, took keen hold, bad mistake 3 out, not recover. **Tommy's Oscar** has been one of the stories of the season over hurdles, but this proved a step too far, not really handling the track and beaten as soon as the tempo lifted; patiently ridden, not settle fully, labouring 3 out. **Teahupoo** beaten just once in 7 races over hurdles below Grade 1 level, ran poorly as he stepped up in class, beaten a long way from home, perhaps needing softer ground to be seen to advantage; waited with, lost place quickly 3 out, eased.

CHELTENHAM Wednesday March 16
Race: 1-5: SOFT, Remainder: HEAVY

Ballymore Novices' Hurdle (Baring Bingham) (Grade 1) (1)

Pos	Btn	Horse	Age	Wgt	Eq	Trainer	Jockey	SP
1		SIR GERHARD (IRE)	7	11-7		W. P. Mullins, Ireland	P. Townend	8/11f
2	3½	THREE STRIPE LIFE (IRE)	6	11-7		Gordon Elliott, Ireland	Davy Russell	8/1
3	9	WHATDEAWANT (IRE)	6	11-7		W. P. Mullins, Ireland	D. E. Mullins	18/1
4	8½	I AM MAXIMUS (FR)	6	11-7		Nicky Henderson	Nico de Boinville	12/1
5	33	HEMLOCK	5	11-7		T. Gibney, Ireland	D. J. O'Keeffe	200/1
6	6	HAXO (FR)	5	11-7		W. P. Mullins, Ireland	S. F. O'Keeffe	125/1
7	4	SCARFACE (IRE)	5	11-7		Colin Tizzard	Brendan Powell	66/1
F		JOURNEY WITH ME (IRE)	6	11-7		Henry de Bromhead, Ireland	Rachael Blackmore	5/1
pu		STAGE STAR (IRE)	6	11-7		Paul Nicholls	Harry Cobden	7/1

9 ran Race Time 5m 21.10 Closing Sectional (4.10f): 61.3s (102.3%) Winning Owner: Cheveley Park Stud

Significant rain, which began in mid-morning and continued throughout the day, made for conditions in marked contrast to the previous day, the rain not forecast, to the extent that the Clerk of the Course had watered parts of the track overnight, the ground soft by the time of this opener, as last season a historically small field lining up, just 3 British stables with a runner, one of those a maiden sent off at 66/1, 2 of the Irish-trained runners at even longer odds, though those at the head of the market set a good standard, the first 3 in the betting unbeaten, none of the field having run more than 3 times over hurdles; Sir Gerhard was following the same owner's Envoi Allen in adding this race to a win in the Champion Bumper, the irony here that the winner had been trained by Gordon Elliott, responsible for the runner-up, until his ban for bringing racing into disrepute last March; the pace was steady early, and several were very keen as a result, the winner among them. **Sir Gerhard** was running here in preference to sticking to 2m, this proving the better option as he'd not have got near Constitution Hill, on the evidence to date, though he's still very promising in his own right, beaten just once in 7 starts, ridden much more patiently over this much longer trip, some doubt on pedigree about his stamina, though he saw the trip out fully, despite not settling when the pace was steady; held up, jumped better than last time, pulled hard, went prominent fourth, led on bridle entering straight, ridden approaching last, edged left, kept on run-in, ridden out; remains open to improvement, his physique suggesting he's very much a chaser, though apparently more thought of as a Champion Hurdle candidate. **Three Stripe Life** finished runner-up in a Grade 1 novice for the third start running, chasing home Sir Gerhard for the second time, having also been behind him in last season's Champion Bumper, having no issue with the longer trip here; held up, travelled well, headway after fourth, mistake seventh, ridden straight, keeping on when left second last, no impression on winner; he's likely to stay further still. **Whatdeawant** had a fair bit to find on form with the principals and showed further improvement, though was unable to go with the leading trio from the second last; close up early, settled in touch third, shaken up 3 out, not quicken next; he's progressed well over hurdles, but looks a chaser and could do even better at that discipline next season. **I Am Maximus** fared best of the British-trained runners, the home team having a poor record in the race in recent years, with just one win since 2013 and not many more placed, though he wasn't a factor in the second half of the race; tracked pace, lost place halfway, pushed along after sixth, weakened 2 out; he's less obviously a chaser in the making than most in this field. **Hemlock** was flying too high in this grade, yet to win a maiden; led, raced freely, headed after fourth, weakened after seventh; he looks the part and may well have a future, particularly as a chaser, at a lower level. **Haxo** upped markedly in trip, was taking a big step up in class after his recent debut win and never threatened to get involved; held up, blundered first, labouring sixth; he lacks the substance at present of many of the others in this field. **Scarface** was an optimistic runner at this level and was nowhere near up to the task; held up, labouring 3 out. **Journey With Me** well backed, was in the process of running well, likely to have finished just behind the runner-up, when he departed at the last, this just the fourth race of his career, so with potential for still more to come over hurdles, though his physique and demeanour very much suggest he'll be an even better chaser; tracked pace, not settle fully, led after fourth, headed entering straight, not quicken, second when fell last. **Stage Star** clearly didn't give his running, his rider reporting the horse as racing too keenly, which was true, though he found nothing off the bridle and his jumping was much less polished than previously, leaving the overall impression that all wasn't well; tracked pace, not always fluent, not settle fully, ridden 3 out, folded tamely, pulled up straight.

Brown Advisory Novices' Chase (Broadway) (Grade 1) (1)

Pos	Btn	Horse	Age	Wgt	Eq	Trainer	Jockey	SP
1		L'HOMME PRESSE (FR)	7	11-4		Venetia Williams	Charlie Deutsch	9/4f
2	3½	AHOY SENOR (IRE)	7	11-4		Lucinda Russell	Derek Fox	4/1
3	1¾	GAILLARD DU MESNIL (FR)	6	11-4		W. P. Mullins, Ireland	P. Townend	11/1
4	7	CAPODANNO (FR)	6	11-4	(t)	W. P. Mullins, Ireland	M. P. Walsh	5/1
5	2	DUSART (IRE)	7	11-4		Nicky Henderson	Nico de Boinville	20/1
6	4¼	THREEUNDERTHRUFIVE (IRE)	7	11-4		Paul Nicholls	A. P. Heskin	14/1
7	9	BEACON EDGE (IRE)	8	11-4	(s)	Noel Meade, Ireland	Sean Flanagan	8/1
F		FAROUK D'ALENE (FR)	7	11-4		Gordon Elliott, Ireland	Davy Russell	9/2
pu		STREETS OF DOYEN (IRE)	8	11-4	(t)	John McConnell, Ireland	S. D. Torrens	150/1

9 ran Race Time 6m 35.80 Closing Sectional (3.75f): 57.40s (106.1%) Winning Owner: DFA Racing (Pink & Edwards)

A heavyweight clash in the Golden Miller only served to strengthen the domestic challenge in this, even with the eleventh-hour withdrawal of Bravemansgame on account of the marked change in conditions from the opening day, though the Irish challenge was a shade underwhelming on paper, particularly with Fury Road, winner of the Fort Leney, also a late absentee; that said, the winner's performance looks up to scratch for the race, his jumping so assured, in contrast to the runner-up, and looking to have matters in hand when Farouk d'Alene—still in second at the time—took a tumble 2 out, his strength at the line fully vindicating the decision to step him up in trip. **L'Homme Presse** fully vindicated connections' decision to run here rather than in the following day's Golden Miller, maintaining his unbeaten record over fences with a most-controlled performance, the quality of his jumping completely belying his novice status, fully proving his stamina for a testing 3m in the process; he travelled well and jumped impeccably, taking him to the front soon after the seventh, was shaken up 2 out but always had matters in hand, feeling the whip only once he began to idle halfway up the run-in, his response as striking as his jumping had been, charging through the line like a horse still some way from his limit in terms of both form and probably stamina too (will relish the Gold Cup trip, for instance); just like Edwardstone the day before, he's a triumph for some quite bold campaigning, this the fifth run of a chasing career that began only at the start of December from a BHA mark of 128. **Ahoy Senor** is probably as talented a novice chaser as there is in training in Britain in terms of raw ability, his runaway win in the Sefton on just his second start over hurdles an indication of that, but his jumping really held him back here, in such vivid contrast to the winner; he avoided major errors for the first two-thirds of the race but did lose the lead soon after he wasn't fluent at the seventh, clouted the fourteenth when still close up and made another pretty bad mistake at a key stage 3 out, began to stay on again approaching the next where he was left second, threatened briefly to really challenge the winner after the last but hung left and could stay on at just one pace; clearly he's capable of running to a higher level still if his jumping improves. **Gaillard du Mesnil** is still to win over fences but produced his best effort to date trying 3m for the first time, and he's got unfinished business as a stayer on the back of this, coming from much further back than the first 2 and hampered by the faller at the second last to boot; held up, crept closer twelfth, closing when had to sidestep the faller 2 out (costing him momentum), untidy last, stayed on, clawing back the gap to Ahoy Senor late on; a year younger than the first 2, he could come back an even stronger contender for this or the National Hunt Chase next year should he retain his novice status. **Capodanno** over 3m for the first time over fences, struggled to get into a rhythm and never really threatened to be more than a bit-part player; held up, awkward sixth, untidy fourteenth, struggling 3 out, some headway next, no further impression. **Dusart** managed to advance his form but at the same time showcased his inexperience (this just the fifth run of his life); mid-field, bad mistake twelfth, pushed along 4 out, no threat from next but finished quite well up the hill to regain fifth; open to further improvement, it's likely he can do some damage next season from a handicap mark that stood at 147 coming into this. **Threeunderthrufive** had won a host of small-field events this winter and came up well short faced with much his stiffest test to date over fences, running in this in preference to the National Hunt Chase after 9 weeks off; chased leaders, pecked ninth, effort after 3 out, faded next. **Beacon Edge** who'd shaped well in the Stayers' Hurdle last year, was closely matched with Farouk d'Alene from the time before but didn't run anywhere near as well as that one; mid-field, not always fluent, lost ground 3 out, no threat after. **Farouk d'Alene** has had a good first season over fences and would likely have emerged best of the Irish but for a late tumble; mid-field early, he pecked at the first and was slow at the second but soon warmed up, chasing the leaders from the eighth and just beginning to be shaken up in second when falling 2 out, rated as finishing just in front of Ahoy Senor. **Streets of Doyen** was back over a suitable trip but was out of his depth; in rear, hit third, clouted seventh, reminders circuit out, lost touch long way out.

Betway Queen Mother Champion Chase (Grade 1) (1)

Pos	Btn	Horse	Age	Wgt	Eq	Trainer	Jockey	SP
1		ENERGUMENE (FR)	8	11-10		W. P. Mullins, Ireland	P. Townend	5/2
2	8½	FUNAMBULE SIVOLA (FR)	7	11-10		Venetia Williams	Charlie Deutsch	40/1
3	4½	ENVOI ALLEN (FR)	8	11-10	(t)	Henry de Bromhead, Ireland	Rachael Blackmore	10/1
4	12	POLITOLOGUE (FR)	11	11-10	(t)	Paul Nicholls	Harry Cobden	80/1
5	2¼	PUT THE KETTLE ON (IRE)	8	11-3	(s)	Henry de Bromhead, Ireland	Aidan Coleman	20/1
ur		CHACUN POUR SOI (FR)	10	11-10		W. P. Mullins, Ireland	Mr P. W. Mullins	8/1
pu		SHISHKIN (IRE)	8	11-10		Nicky Henderson	Nico de Boinville	5/6f

7 ran Race Time 4m 06.70 Closing Sectional (3.75f): 58.1s (100.1%) Winning Owner: Tony Bloom

One of the most anticipated clashes of the week, a rematch between Shishkin and Energumene following their epic battle in the Clarence House, Chacun Pour Soi another arriving at the top of his game, the race on paper a much stronger contest than either of the last 2 runnings, hence the long odds at which the winners of those, Politlogue and Put The Kettle On, were sent off; the race failed totally to deliver, however, only one of the 3 market leaders completing, he landing the spoils under a change of tactics. **Energumene** under a change of tactics, landed the first of what may well be many Grade 1s outside novice company, pulling clear on the run-in, though with his main rivals out of contention he didn't have to run quite to his best to do so; held up, not fluent second, headway ninth, led on bridle 2 out, in command soon after, kept up to work; he's sure to win more good races, though hopefully Shishkin and Chacun Pour Soi will give him something to think about should they meet again. **Funambule Sivola** up in grade, proved better than ever, sticking to his task willingly having travelled as if well at home at this level, the Melling at Aintree an option, should connections want to return to further; held up, travelled well, upsides 4 out, shaken up home turn, kept on run-in, no match for winner. **Envoi Allen** had been sent off at 2/1, 4/7 and 4/6 on 3 previous Festival visits, with wins in the Champion Bumper and Baring Bingham to his name, but things haven't gone to plan since his early departure last season and, though he'd won a Grade 1 last time, he'd had another breathing operation since and didn't fully see the race out, that he's being campaigned at 2m after spending most of his career over further a negative in itself; disputed lead early, remained prominent, led before 3 out, headed when blundered next, no extra run-in. **Politologue** winner of this race in 2020, as well as a Melling Chase and the Tingle Creek twice, was well held after 4 months off, a grand servant to connections over a long career, his debut coming nearly 7 years previously, and now heading off to retirement; in touch, left behind from 3 out. **Put The Kettle On** twice a winner at this meeting, looks rather out of sorts with the game at the moment and failed to revive for the fitting of headgear, geed up beforehand; handy, pressed leader early final circuit, left in front ninth, headed before 3 out, left behind soon after. **Chacun Pour Soi** hadn't been seen at his best in 2 previous visits to Britain, so it was frustrating that he didn't get the chance to put the record straight, departing after a rare jumping lapse; led until blundered and unseated rider ninth. **Shishkin** was a massive disappointment, connections blaming the ground, though he gave such a lethargic performance, beaten almost from the off, that there was surely something more to it than that; held up, jumped ponderously, never travelling well, pulled up after eighth; hopefully he can bounce back next time, with time to recover for either Punchestown or Sandown.

Weatherbys Champion Bumper (Standard Open National Hunt Flat) (Grade 1) (1)

Pos	Btn	Horse	Age	Wgt	Eq	Trainer	Jockey	SP
1		FACILE VEGA (IRE)	5	11-5		W. P. Mullins, Ireland	Mr P. W. Mullins	15/8f
2	3¾	AMERICAN MIKE (IRE)	5	11-5		Gordon Elliott, Ireland	Mr J. J. Codd	5/2
3	2½	JAMES'S GATE (IRE)	5	11-5		W. P. Mullins, Ireland	S. F. O'Keeffe	16/1
4	2¾	SEABANK BISTRO (IRE)	5	11-5		W. P. Mullins, Ireland	B. Hayes	18/1
5	1¾	AUTHORISED SPEED (FR)	5	11-5		Gary Moore	Joshua Moore	50/1
6	2¼	POETIC MUSIC	4	10-2		Fergal O'Brien	Paddy Brennan	33/1
7	¾	OUR JESTER	6	11-5		Hughie Morrison	Nico de Boinville	50/1
8	4½	MUSIC DRIVE (FR)	5	11-5	(t)	Gordon Elliott, Ireland	Davy Russell	50/1
9	8½	SPANISH PRESENT (IRE)	6	11-5		Martin Keighley	Sean Bowen	250/1
10	hd	VIVA DEVITO (IRE)	5	11-5	(h)	W. P. Mullins, Ireland	Mr D. O'Connor	25/1
11	10	MADMANSGAME	5	11-5		W. P. Mullins, Ireland	D. E. Mullins	10/1
12	8½	CILLIANS CHARM (IRE)	5	11-5		Anthony McCann, Ireland	Jonathan Moore	250/1
13	20	REDEMPTION DAY	5	11-5		W. P. Mullins, Ireland	P. Townend	7/1
14	¾	OCEAN OF MERCY (IRE)	6	11-5		Paul Hennessy, Ireland	Sam Twiston-Davies	125/1
15	41	HOULANBATORDECHAIS (FR)	5	11-5		W. P. Mullins, Ireland	Rachael Blackmore	14/1
pu		AIN'T NO SUNSHINE (IRE)	6	11-5		Keith Dalgleish	Danny McMenamin	125/1
pu		CALL ME HARRY (IRE)	5	11-5		Iain Jardine	Conor O'Farrell	125/1
pu		GODOT (IRE)	5	11-5		Andy Irvine	Brendan Powell	250/1
pu		JOYEUX MACHIN (FR)	5	11-5	(t)	Paul Nolan, Ireland	B. J. Cooper	33/1
pu		TOP DOG (IRE)	5	11-5		Emma Lavelle	Tom Bellamy	50/1

20 ran   Race Time 4m 06.10   Closing Sectional (4.10f): 59.60s (103.2%)   Winning Owner: Hammer & Trowel Syndicate

Perhaps the most testing conditions ever for the Champion Bumper, though the time was a fraction faster than that recorded by Ferny Hollow in 2020, the start of the race delayed while the course was reconfigured, several of the hurdles positions having to be bypassed due to the incessant rain, that 5 of the longshots were pulled up testament to the testing nature of the race, though the principals saw things out well, the form shown by the winner well up to standard for the race, his performance as good as any since probably Briar Hill in 2013, another of now 12 winners in the contest for Willie Mullins, who fielded 7 runners, 6 of them unbeaten, 3 making the frame, only American Mike breaking the stable stranglehold, British yards mustering just 8 runners, none of them sent off at shorter than 33/1, though the 4 that finished acquitted themselves with credit, the field overall one of the most impressive on looks in recent years. **Facile Vega** was clearly his stable's no.1 candidate, from a team of 7, and won in the style of a very good prospect indeed, in form terms one of the best of his stable's 12 winners of this race, looks and pedigree making the mouth water too, no surprise to see him back as a hot favourite for, perhaps, the Baring Bingham in 12 months; held up, travelled strongly, smooth headway 3f out, led entering straight, in command soon after, won readily. **American Mike** did everything he could, confirming himself as a smart novice hurdling prospect for next season; held up, travelled well, good progress end of back straight, led 4f out, ridden entering straight, headed soon after, kept on, no match for winner. **James's Gate** about the pick of the whole field on looks, had handled testing conditions well at Punchestown and was much improved from that debut, stepped up in class; in touch, travelled well, good progress 3f out, chased leaders straight, kept on; like the others in the frame, he surely has a very bright future. **Seabank Bistro** down in trip, was helped by the emphasis on stamina and improved from debut, plenty to like about him physically and sure to have a bright future over jumps; held up, travelled well, headway end of back straight, every chance 3f out, not quicken over 1f out. **Authorised Speed** ran well, up in grade, suited by the way the race developed and emerging best of the home team, the type that will win races over hurdles for his excellent yard next season; held up, headway over 4f out, every chance 3f out, shaken up home turn, one paced. **Poetic Music** ran creditably, taking on her elders for the first time, ridden in similar fashion to previously, the tactics perhaps a little overdone; dropped out, still plenty to do over 3f out, kept on well straight, nearest at the finish. **Our Jester** ran creditably upped in grade, plenty of experience to draw on; in touch, effort 3f out, not quicken, kept on final 1f; he has the physique for hurdling, though his pedigree might suggest a career on the Flat. **Music Drive** ran creditably, in a much more competitive contest than previously, looking a stayer; handy, outpaced over 3f out, kept on final 1f, edged left. **Spanish Present** ran about as well as could have been expected upped in grade, doing better than most of those ridden to the fore; prominent, shaken up over 3f out, weakened home turn; he's not at all a bad type and ought to have a future as a jumper. **Viva Devito** after 3 months off, was flying a bit too high in this grade, but there's a fair bit to like about him as a type and he's another to make a novice hurdler next season; held up, not settle fully, some headway 4f out, left behind home turn. **Madmansgame** went backwards from debut, just 3 weeks on, doing a bit too much in front in a race dominated at the finish by those held up; took keen hold, led until halfway, remained prominent, every chance 4f out, weakened soon after; he's an imposing sort with a good pedigree and seems sure to make an impact as a novice hurdler next season. **Cillians Charm** was flying too high in this grade, after just the one run at Catterick, on the weak side at present as well; tracked pace early, lost place completely after 3f, ridden end of back straight, left behind 3f out. **Redemption Day** after 11 weeks off, went backwards from debut, towards the head of the stable pecking order, judged on jockey bookings and the market, but failing to show the abundant promise of his debut, one of few to stay on the inside down the hill, though the third was there as well; in touch, not settle fully, weakened 3f out; looks, pedigree and debut win all suggest he's worth another chance to confirm that promise. **Ocean of Mercy** was well held after 5 months off, conditions much more testing than previously, though with a lot to find at this level anyway; prominent, labouring end of back straight, weakened soon after, tailed off. **Houlanbatordechais** bought for €150,000 after winning both starts in France for Alain Couetil, had steering problems after 5 months off, pulling so hard that the bit slipped through his mouth; handy, refused to settle, hung right back straight, led halfway, headed 4f out, soon done with, tailed off. **Ain't No Sunshine** ran no sort of race, up in grade; held up, soon off bridle, tailed off end of back straight, pulled up. **Call Me Harry** faced a stiff task, despite having won his 2 previous races, but probably just didn't cope with much softer ground; waited with, took keen hold, labouring before halfway, tailed off when pulled up before straight. **Godot** was well out of his depth; close up, not settle fully, weakened quickly end of back straight, tailed off when pulled up before straight. **Joyeux Machin** was flying too high in this grade; held up, headway early final circuit, labouring after halfway, pulled up over 3f out. **Top Dog** presumably failed to handle much softer ground, his form last time, with the fifth here behind him, good enough to see him run close to the best of the home team at least; prominent, weakened over 4f out, tailed off when pulled up straight.

CHELTENHAM Thursday March 17
GOOD to SOFT

Turners Novices' Chase (Golden Miller) (Grade 1) (1)

Pos	Btn	Horse	Age	Wgt	Eq	Trainer	Jockey	SP
1		BOB OLINGER (IRE)	7	11-4		Henry de Bromhead, Ireland	Rachael Blackmore	6/5
2	40	BUSSELTON (FR)	5	11-2		Joseph Patrick O'Brien, Ireland	J. J. Slevin	50/1
3	28	EL BARRA (FR)	8	11-4		W. P. Mullins, Ireland	Mr P. W. Mullins	18/1
F		GALOPIN DES CHAMPS (FR)	6	11-4		W. P. Mullins, Ireland	P. Townend	5/6f

4 ran Race Time 5m 08.00 Closing Sectional (3.84f): 65.10s (91.9%) Winning Owner: Robcour

An anti-climax to an anti-climax, as the smallest Festival field in decades—and one completely free of British representation—failed to produce the thrilling division-deciding match that might well have been able to save it, a lacklustre Bob Olinger having no answer to his big rival when Galopin des Champs stood so far off the last he knuckled over on landing, handing it to a most fortunate winner. **Bob Olinger** made it 3-3 over fences, 6 wins in a row all told and 2 successes from as many Festival visits, yet this was a performance that raised question marks rather than acted as a further step closer to the top of the chasing tree, needing extreme luck on his side after Galopin des Champs had left him trailing from 3 out (had got gap back to a couple of lengths after losing ground by hitting fence prior), hanging left and carrying his head awkwardly under full pressure and unable to respond—11 lengths down and beaten—when left clear at the last, hitting the line with no verve at all; clearly, it's just possible he was up against one out of the very top drawer, but his jumping was cautious/awkward at times and, much like Ahoy Senor the previous day, needs to iron out those flaws if he's to scale the expected heights in open company next season; perhaps reinventing him as a hurdler is the right long-term move. **Busselton** had no chance with the front 2 but, testament to the favourite's strong-running style, was still taken out of his comfort zone further out than might have been expected, struggling early on the final circuit having jumped with caution at times. **El Barra** is a useful novice but was merely making up the numbers in this field out again 4 days after Limerick; held up, went third fifth, struggling when jumped right tenth. **Galopin des Champs** found himself in against a misfiring Bob Olinger as it turned out but still put his name alongside the likes of Goshen and Annie Power as recent Cheltenham Festival certainties who left with nothing to show for it, galloping and jumping (stood off and hit the eighth, admittedly) in a fashion that had the also-rans flat out from halfway and, after his main rival had recovered from a blunder to close the gap to a couple of lengths 3 out, opening right up again on the home turn, extending his lead to 11 lengths by the time he buckled on landing having been asked to go long at the last, likely to have won by a margin at least half as far again; he's the best novice chaser in training.

Ryanair Chase (Festival Trophy) (Grade 1) (1)

Pos	Btn	Horse	Age	Wgt	Eq	Trainer	Jockey	SP
1		ALLAHO (FR)	8	11-10	(t)	W. P. Mullins, Ireland	P. Townend	4/7f
2	14	JANIDIL (FR)	8	11-10		W. P. Mullins, Ireland	M. P. Walsh	12/1
3	¾	ELDORADO ALLEN (FR)	8	11-10	(t)	Colin Tizzard	Brendan Powell	14/1
4	13	FANION D'ESTRUVAL (FR)	7	11-10		Venetia Williams	Charlie Deutsch	28/1
5	2¾	MELON	10	11-10	(s)	W. P. Mullins, Ireland	Mr P. W. Mullins	16/1
6	1¼	SHAN BLUE (IRE)	8	11-10		Dan Skelton	Harry Skelton	10/1
F		CONFLATED (IRE)	8	11-10		Gordon Elliott, Ireland	Davy Russell	7/1

7 ran Race Time 5m 10.50 Closing Sectional (3.84f): 60.40s (95.9%) Winning Owner: Cheveley Park Stud

The most one-sided race of the Festival in terms of betting and it panned out that way in the event, too, with Allaho repeating his 2021 win with another imperious front-running display, his performance a near-identical one both in style and substance to twelve months earlier; the pace was good. **Allaho** is clearly one of the best horses in training and is now unbeaten on his last 5 starts at around 2½m, the intermediate trip suiting his free-wheeling style down to the ground—indeed, this latest victory was every bit as good in terms of form as his stunning win in last year's renewal, the only threat to him in the short term likely to come from within his own stable; made all, typically went with zest/jumped superbly in main, quickened clear from home turn, in control when untidy last, impressive. **Janidil** ran respectably back down in trip, just not in the same league as his top-notch stable-companion for all that he got within 2 lengths of him earlier in the campaign; waited with, crept closer from halfway, went second early in straight, plugged on. **Eldorado Allen** is a likeable sort who's held his form well this season, arguably deserving extra credit here for trying to mix it with Allaho for so long—previous comments about the 25f Bowl being his best Aintree option remain; chased leader, jumped well, lost second early in straight, rallied. **Fanion d'Estruval** made little impact in this race for the second successive year and, acknowledging last month's Ascot Chase third, isn't really up to strong Grade 1 company; dropped out, mistake water jump, merely passed beaten horses late on. **Melon** possibly isn't quite the force of old and disappointed back in Grade 1 company, this second successive below-par Ryanair Chase display putting a dent into his otherwise impressive Cheltenham Festival record (runner-up 4 times); mid-division, blundered fifth, left behind from 5 out. **Shan Blue** almost certainly isn't so good as his striking Charlie Hall display implied and he was well held after 5 months off, though connections' disappointment should be tempered by the knowledge they still have the option of exploiting his BHA mark of just 148 back in valuable handicap company; mid-division, typically travelled well, in contention 4 out, brushed aside from home turn. **Conflated** went a long way to backing up last month's surprise Irish Gold Cup win and clearly belongs at Grade 1 level; soon behind, plenty to do halfway, not fluent tenth, rapid headway from 4 out, keeping on in a share of second (albeit no match for winner) when fell heavily 2 out.

Paddy Power Stayers' Hurdle (Grade 1) (1)

Pos	Btn	Horse	Age	Wgt	Eq	Trainer	Jockey	SP
1		FLOORING PORTER (IRE)	7	11-10	(t)	Gavin Patrick Cromwell, Ireland	D. E. Mullins	4/1
2	2¾	THYME HILL	8	11-10		Philip Hobbs	Tom O'Brien	11/2
3	ns	PAISLEY PARK (IRE)	10	11-10	(t)	Emma Lavelle	Aidan Coleman	17/2
4	1¼	CHAMP (IRE)	10	11-10		Nicky Henderson	Jonjo O'Neill Jr.	11/2
5	1	KLASSICAL DREAM (FR)	8	11-10	(h)	W. P. Mullins, Ireland	P. Townend	11/4f
6	2½	HOME BY THE LEE (IRE)	7	11-10		Joseph Patrick O'Brien, Ireland	J. J. Slevin	33/1
7	nk	KOSHARI (FR)	10	11-10	(s)	David Christie, Ireland	Jonathan Moore	100/1
8	¾	ROYAL KAHALA (IRE)	7	11-3		Peter Fahey, Ireland	K. C. Sexton	11/2
9	5½	SONG FOR SOMEONE (GER)	7	11-10		Tom Symonds	Nico de Boinville	33/1
pu		LISNAGAR OSCAR (IRE)	9	11-10	(s)	Rebecca Curtis	Adam Wedge	40/1

10 ran Race Time 5m 59.20 Closing Sectional (3.7f): 55.7s (99.5%) Winning Owner: Flooring Porter Syndicate

Fitting circumstances for the seasonal showpiece of a staying division about which more had been made of the potential for a fun-and-games start than the overall merit of a scene lacking the powerhouse names of the past, Flooring Porter the beneficiary of Klassical Dream's misstep as the tapes were released this time and able to secure an even more hassle-free lead than he had in the race in 2021 as he became the latest multiple winner of the Stayers', not that his Timeform rating can be placed close to such tip-toppers as Baracouda, Inglis Drever and Big Buck's to have achieved the feat before, the proximity of Home By The Lee and Koshari in a bunched finish very much supporting a cautious stance. **Flooring Porter** had the start go his way this time as he became the latest back-to-back winner of this premier staying prize, though he isn't in the same mould—for ability or style—as the likes of Big Buck's and Inglis Drever, benefiting from an uncontested lead for the second year in a row (old rival Klassical Dream missed break) and, aided by the sort of slick hurdling normally reserved for leading 2-milers, not having to exert himself until the run-in, the ride so well judged and his lead so soft that Mullins didn't even have to resort to the whip as he dismissed the favourite's brief threat from the last, reducing arrears in their still inconclusive private battle to 2-1; he blew out totally behind Klassical Dream at Punchestown following his win here last season. **Thyme Hill** has seen a potential climb to the top of the staying tree stall somewhat but emerged with credit in finishing second at the highest level yet again 13 weeks on from the Long Walk, especially as he found himself less-than-ideally placed in a tactical race, pushed along to make his headway through the bunched field entering the straight and just holding the late surge of his old adversary Paisley Park for second, the well-ridden winner beyond reach; he'll be bang there again at Aintree if bidding to follow up his Liverpool Hurdle win next month. **Paisley Park** might have lost a step in terms of ability but everything else about him is just as it's always been since his rise through the staying ranks carried him to success in this race in such stirring fashion in 2019, finishing third behind Flooring Porter for the second year in a row but deserving extra credit for it this time around given the false pace and long-time congested field wasn't in his favour, still outpaced with only one behind him on the home turn before he began to motor, all but carrying him to second. **Champ** hasn't quite kicked on from his Long Walk defeat of Thyme Hill and Paisley Park as might have been expected, rather too lit up this time to deliver the finish that he promised, a stronger pace likely to have suited him as indeed it would that reopposing pair; waited with, took strong hold, took closer order after 3 out, threatened entering straight, pushed along approaching last, one paced. **Klassical Dream** went a long way to erasing the memory of the Galmoy having been freshened up since but, in a reversal of fortunes from their meeting at Christmas, found himself on the wrong side of a ragged start that saw Flooring Porter get the jump this time, forced into a much more patient ride and easing through to close the gap to little more than a length as he crossed the last only to land awkwardly and find no extra, even run out of the frame; all things being equal, which as yet it hasn't been for differing reasons in his 3 clashes with Flooring Porter, there'll be next to nothing between them at Punchestown. **Home By The Lee** seemed to run above himself by an even bigger margin but owed plenty to a messy race for all he's clearly at his very best as a staying hurdler these days; in touch, lost ground between 3 out and 2 out, not quicken approaching last, stayed on again final 50 yds. **Koshari** ran about as well as could have been expected upped in grade after 4 months off, unable to make the same headway from rear as the bigger guns ahead; dropped out, crept closer from 2 out, no further impression. **Royal Kahala** didn't have the chance the market suggested at this level after 7 weeks off but nor did she give the impression she was at her very best, unusually weak in the finish having turned in still bang there, no response running to the last. **Song For Someone** failed to improve for a much different trip but will have more chance of proving his worth as a stayer in calmer waters, that or he's simply one of those lazy customers regardless of trip; waited with, out wide, slow fourth, headway under pressure briefly 2 out, effort proved short-lived. **Lisnagar Oscar** followed a better run (behind the third/fourth here) with a poor one, adding to a hit-and-miss record; tracked pace out wide until 3 out, struggling before next.

CHELTENHAM Friday March 18
GOOD to SOFT

Jcb Triumph Hurdle (Grade 1) (1)

Pos	Btn	Horse	Age	Wgt	Eq	Trainer	Jockey	SP
1		VAUBAN (FR)	4	11-0	(t)	W. P. Mullins, Ireland	P. Townend	6/4f
2	2½	FIL DOR (FR)	4	11-0		Gordon Elliott, Ireland	Davy Russell	11/2
3	nk	PIED PIPER	4	11-0		Gordon Elliott, Ireland	J. W. Kennedy	7/2
4	4¾	ICARE ALLEN (FR)	4	11-0	(t)	W. P. Mullins, Ireland	M. P. Walsh	10/1
5	1¼	IL ETAIT TEMPS (FR)	4	11-0		W. P. Mullins, Ireland	D. E. Mullins	12/1
6	2¼	PORTICELLO (FR)	4	11-0		Gary Moore	Jamie Moore	8/1
7	¾	DOCTOR PARNASSUS (IRE)	4	11-0		Dan Skelton	Harry Skelton	25/1
8	4½	LUNAR POWER (IRE)	4	11-0	(s)	Noel Meade, Ireland	Sean Flanagan	80/1
9	3¾	KNIGHT SALUTE	4	11-0	(h)	Milton Harris	Paddy Brennan	16/1
10	5	TEDDY BLUE (GER)	4	11-0	(h)	Gary Moore	Joshua Moore	40/1
11	3½	KOI DODVILLE (FR)	4	11-0	(b)	David Pipe	Tom Scudamore	200/1
12	27	AGES OF MAN (IRE)	4	11-0		Anthony McCann, Ireland	Jonathan Moore	200/1

12 ran Race Time 4m 06.90 Closing Sectional (3.70f): 51.8s (104.9%) Winning Owner: Mrs S. Ricci

A race that set the tone for a day of total Irish domination, the first 5 home all trained there, as were all 7 winners on the day, with the home team managing to make the frame just twice in the 3 Grade 1 events, several of the main British-trained hopes performing dismally; as for the Triumph itself, the field finished rather too close together to take a particularly high view, the winner's performance no more than around average of those over the last decade, the race developing from the second last, the winner able to grab the rail in the straight, as his rider did in the following race as well, though he was clearly on the best horse and any advantage in that position was not the difference between winning and losing; the Spring Juvenile Hurdle, as so often in recent years, proved the key trial, the first 2 there filling the same positions here. **Vauban** confirmed the promise of his win in the Spring Juvenile, showing again a good turn of foot, indeed having to do so twice after fluffing the last, likely to have won by a bit further and with even more in hand without that, clearly the most promising of these, even if a single-figure quote for the 2023 Champion Hurdle looks skinny, this form light years away from what Constitution Hill achieved in the Supreme, his jumping not as polished as likely to be required for the best open company, the record of the Triumph as a Champion Hurdle pointer in any case pretty ropey in recent times (though this year's Champion third Zanahiyr filled the same position in this last season); handy, not fluent second, led on bridle before last, in control when not fluent there, shaken up after, quickened clear final 100 yds, won readily; open to further improvement and likely to make an impact in good races in open company. **Fil Dor** the most experienced of the first 3, had been done for foot by the winner at Leopardstown and it was the same story on a stiffer track, likely to be seen to at least as good advantage over further, that perhaps his best route to success next season; pressed leader, travelled well, edged ahead after 2 out, shaken up straight, headed before last, left behind by winner final 100 yds. **Pied Piper** acquitted himself well, plenty to like about the way he's taken to hurdling, like the winner having just his third start at this discipline, physically the type who should hold his own in open company next season, a good win this spring potentially there, kept away from the winner; waited with, travelled well, headway 2 out, every chance before last, left behind by winner final 100 yds. **Icare Allen** couldn't find the improvement required to get on terms with a pair that had beaten him in the Spring Juvenile, though he ran creditably and has potential longer term, judged on physique and pedigree, likely to make a chaser in time; prominent, travelled well, not fluent third, shaken up straight, not quicken approaching last. **Il Etait Temps** lacked experience, after just the one run over hurdles, highly promising as that was, and he ran to just a similar level, too keen for his own good early on; handy, pulled hard, mistake first, shaken up straight, challenged before last, one paced; he's shown more than enough to suggest he can win races, highly tried as he has been so far. **Porticello** emerged best of the British-trained runners, though he looked a bit short of pace and might well have done better had this been held on the second day, when the ground was more testing; led, shaken up 2 out, headed soon after, outpaced home turn, plugged on run-in; he's ready for a step up in trip, and may yet do better when he does so. **Doctor Parnassus** was unbeaten in 2 starts over hurdles, but this was a significant step up in class and he wasn't able to make much impact, this perhaps a step too far at this stage; held up, steady headway before 2 out, shaken up straight, effort flattened out. **Lunar Power** had been beaten a fair way by Fil Dor when last seen and found this company too hot, tried in cheekpieces; waited with, shaken up after 2 out, made no impression. **Knight Salute** came into this unbeaten, including in 3 Grade 2 events, but he looked outclassed in the paddock and the race, performing below the level he'd shown against domestic opposition on his last 2 starts; held up, took keen hold, not fluent fifth, ridden after 2 out, made no impression; he's done very well as a juvenile, but lacks scope and may well be hard to place next season. **Teddy Blue** in first-time hood, failed to repeat the form of his second in the Adonis, looking as if still in need of experience, a mistake just as the race was taking shape not helping his cause; held up, not settle fully, still plenty to do approaching 2 out, mistake there, ridden and soon left behind; he may well confirm himself a useful young hurdler in calmer waters. **Koi Dodville** had done nothing to justify his place in this field and was soon put in his place once the race developed; held up, pushed along 3 out, left behind next. **Ages of Man** a maiden after 2 starts over hurdles, was out of his depth; soon behind, tailed off after 2 out.

Albert Bartlett Novices' Hurdle (Spa) (Grade 1) (1)

Pos	Btn	Horse	Age	Wgt	Eq	Trainer	Jockey	SP
1		THE NICE GUY (IRE)	7	11-8		W. P. Mullins, Ireland	S. F. O'Keeffe	18/1
2	5	MINELLA COCOONER (IRE)	6	11-8	(h)	W. P. Mullins, Ireland	P. Townend	9/2
3	4¼	BARDENSTOWN LAD	7	11-8		John McConnell, Ireland	Sean Bowen	20/1
4	4	BALLYGRIFINCOTTAGE (IRE)	7	11-8		Dan Skelton	Harry Skelton	28/1
5	5	GREEN BOOK (FR)	5	11-8		Venetia Williams	Charlie Deutsch	40/1
6	2	RAMILLIES (IRE)	7	11-8	(t)	W. P. Mullins, Ireland	B. J. Cooper	28/1
7	2¼	MAHLER MISSION (IRE)	6	11-8	(t)	John McConnell, Ireland	James Bowen	66/1
8	3¾	BRORSON (IRE)	6	11-8		Martin Keighley	Jamie Moore	100/1
9	16	GOOD TIME JONNY (IRE)	7	11-8	(t)	A. J. Martin, Ireland	K. C. Sexton	12/1
10	9½	SHANTREUSSE (IRE)	6	11-8		Henry de Bromhead, Ireland	Rachael Blackmore	12/1
11	33	ERIC BLOODAXE (IRE)	7	11-8	(t)	Joseph Patrick O'Brien, Ireland	J. J. Slevin	50/1

pu	CLASSIC GETAWAY (IRE)	6	11-8		W. P. Mullins, Ireland	Mr P. W. Mullins	22/1
pu	GINTO (FR)	6	11-8		Gordon Elliott, Ireland	J. W. Kennedy	5/2
pu	HILLCREST (IRE)	7	11-8		Henry Daly	Richard Patrick	9/4f
pu	STAG HORN	5	11-8	(s)	Archie Watson	Nick Scholfield	22/1
pu	WHERE IT ALL BEGAN (IRE)	6	11-8		Gordon Elliott, Ireland	A. P. Heskin	150/1

16 ran Race Time 5m 54.40 Closing Sectional (3.70f): 56.0s (97.7%) Winning Owner: Mr Malcolm C. Denmark

A different test from the sort of pottering around in lesser races that most of the runners in this had experienced, and as so often it produced a winner at a double-figure price, though an unbeaten runner who was only that as the perceived stable second—or third-string, a big step up in trip proving right up his street, the race becoming a real slog late on, dour stayers taking third and fourth, 2 of the runners treated for post-race ataxia, the form of a similar standard to recent runnings; the race was marred by a fatal injury to Ginto when in contention in the straight, while the main British hope Hillcrest ran no race at all, his performance as sluggish as Shishkin's in the Champion Chase. **The Nice Guy** upped markedly in trip, showed much improved form, far from typical of winners of this race, this just his second start over hurdles, clearly a good prospect for all that he wasn't the most obvious of his stable's runners on jockey bookings; patiently ridden, travelled well, headway 3 out, loomed up after next, led last, kept on well, asserted final 100 yds; type to improve further and should make a smart novice chaser next season. **Minella Cocooner** ran well in defeat, much more involved at the head of affairs than the winner, that perhaps the difference between them, still a useful prospect for chasing next season; prominent, travelled well, disputed lead fifth, bad mistake eighth, kicked on 2 out, headed last, not quicken final 100 yds. **Bardenstown Lad** ran well upped in grade, looking a real sluggard, as he had when winning here in the autumn; chased leaders early, lost place fifth, labouring halfway, kept on well after 2 out, took third last; he has the physique to make a chaser, though with a touch of the slows he'll need long distances to be seen to advantage. **Ballygrifincottage** ran well upped in grade, looking suited by the emphasis on stamina, doing well given his lack of experience, a raw-boned type and more a chaser than hurdler on looks; in rear, labouring 3 out, headway next, chased leaders before last, plugged on. **Green Book** wasted no time getting back to form, another from his yard to run at least creditably this week, one of just 2 British-trained runners in the first 7, his effort just petering out late on, reported to be suffering from post-race ataxia; held up, not fluent eighth, still plenty to do 2 out, headway briefly early in straight, no extra last. **Ramillies** upped markedly in trip, didn't quite get home, a combination of going freely and jumping errors finding him out; held up, mistakes first and seventh, shaken up after 3 out, headway approaching straight, chased leaders before last, another mistake there, weakened run-in; he's a strapping sort, every inch a chaser, and hopefully he will jump fences better than he does hurdles. **Mahler Mission** is Irish-trained but represented British form and that proved inadequate in this company; in touch, pushed along after 3 out, lost place soon after; he's likely to make a novice chaser of a decent standard next season, judged on physique and pedigree. **Brorson** had a lot to find on form and ran about as well as could have been expected upped in grade, giving way only in the straight (treated for post-race ataxia); in touch, close up halfway, shaken up before 2 out, weakened approaching last. **Good Time Jonny** was below form, the step up from handicap to Grade 1 novice company proving beyond him; held up, some headway before 2 out, left behind before last. **Shantreusse** had looked a thorough stayer in his 2 wins, so his weakening in the latter stages was especially hard to fathom; prominent, every chance 2 out, weakened approaching last. **Eric Bloodaxe** was well held, facing a stiff task in this company and never competitive, his jumping again found wanting; soon behind, jumped none too fluently, labouring halfway, tailed off 2 out. **Classic Getaway** was amiss, beaten well before the longer trip came into play (bred to stay), his physique, like so many of these, that of a chaser; led until fourth, led again before sixth, headed seventh, weakened quickly, pulled up 3 out, reportedly bled. **Ginto** met a sad end; handy, effort when went wrong early in straight, suffered fatal injury. **Hillcrest** held leading form claims and had shown abundant stamina, but he ran no sort of race, perhaps a slog through the mud at Haydock having left its mark, though still an exciting chasing prospect for next season; jumped off prominently, but almost immediately off the pace, jumped none too fluently, never travelling well, pulled up before 3 out. **Stag Horn** upped in trip and grade, found the company beyond him; close up, not fluent third, led fourth, wandered approaching fifth, headed before sixth, left behind before 3 out, pulled up. **Where It All Began** had a lot to find on form and wasn't up to the task, likely to make more impact as a chaser next season; held up, ridden when blundered 3 out, left behind soon after, pulled up.

Boodles Cheltenham Gold Cup Chase (Grade 1) (1)

Pos	Btn	Horse	Age	Wgt	Eq	Trainer	Jockey	SP
1		A PLUS TARD (FR)	8	11-10	(t)	Henry de Bromhead, Ireland	Rachael Blackmore	3/1f
2	15	MINELLA INDO (IRE)	9	11-10		Henry de Bromhead, Ireland	Robbie Power	7/1
3	2½	PROTEKTORAT (FR)	7	11-10	(t)	Dan Skelton	Harry Skelton	10/1
4	sh	GALVIN (IRE)	8	11-10		Gordon Elliott, Ireland	Davy Russell	10/3
5	nk	ROYALE PAGAILLE (FR)	8	11-10		Venetia Williams	Charlie Deutsch	20/1
6	2¾	AL BOUM PHOTO (FR)	10	11-10	(s)	W. P. Mullins, Ireland	P. Townend	6/1
7	1	ASTERION FORLONGE (FR)	8	11-10	(t)	W. P. Mullins, Ireland	B. J. Cooper	22/1
8	9½	SANTINI	10	11-10		Polly Gundry	Nick Scholfield	66/1
9	30	AYE RIGHT (IRE)	9	11-10		H Graham & G Rutherford	Callum Bewley	80/1
pu		TORNADO FLYER (IRE)	9	11-10		W. P. Mullins, Ireland	D. E. Mullins	9/1
pu		CHANTRY HOUSE (IRE)	8	11-10	(s)	Nicky Henderson	Nico de Boinville	16/1

11 ran Race Time 6m 42.30 Closing Sectional (3.84f): 57.4s (102.3%) Winning Owner: Cheveley Park Stud

A representative field for the Cheltenham Gold Cup, lacking really only the winner of the Irish Gold Cup Conflated, and it looked an open contest beforehand, with not a lot to choose between the pick of the field on their best form, a close contest continuing to look on the cards for much of the way, the pace ordinary on the first circuit, plenty still with a chance and going okay 3 out, the winner in a bit of a pocket as last season's winner Minella Indo kicked for home, before he picked up in the straight and stormed up the run-in in remarkable fashion, the winning margin the widest in the race since Master Oats scored by the same distance in the mud in 1995, the winner's superiority over the second somewhat exaggerated, his stable companion finishing rather tamely, though clearly A Plus Tard deserves his place at the head of the staying chasing pecking order. **A Plus Tard** went one better than last season, storming home after a close contest had looked on the cards entering the straight, this performance, along with his win in the Betfair Chase, clearly showing him the best of the staying chasers, though perhaps not so far ahead of the rest as the margins in the 2 races might suggest; held up, travelled well, shaken up 3 out, short of room entering straight, went second 2 out, led last, stayed on strongly; he didn't run again last season after the Gold Cup or the season before after the Ryanair, and disappointed when he did take in the Punchestown Festival prior to that, so it remains to be seen if he runs again this spring and whether he can back up this excellent effort in the short term. **Minella Indo** added another second place to his excellent Festival record, and he clearly emerges with credit, though he didn't finish the race nearly so well as looked likely after he quickened off the bend, 3 defeats after trading short-in-running now along with his King George flop on his return this season something of a concern; in touch, travelled well, chased leaders 4 out, led next, quickened clear home turn, ridden early in straight, headed when mistake last, no extra run-in. **Protektorat** ran well after 3 months off, seeing the slightly longer trip out and emerging best of the British, a year younger than any of his rivals and likely to be a contender again next season, though the Bowl at Aintree might well offer more immediate compensation; held up, travelled well, effort before 3 out, chased leader early in straight, one paced, beaten when blundered last. **Galvin** who had beaten the winner in the Savills and had won the NH Chase here last season, ran respectably, just wanting for pace at a crucial stage; held up, mistake fifteenth, ridden 4 out, short of room after, outpaced approaching home turn, stayed on again run-in. **Royale Pagaille** gave a much better account of himself than he had as a novice in this race last season, though presumably even softer ground would have helped him still further, still young enough for a third serious crack at the race next season, though a Betfair Chase in the mud might be his ideal option, his performance another fine one from the stable which, along with Nicky Henderson's, that did best of the British during the week; held up, went prominent ninth, every chance when clouted 4 out, outpaced entering straight. **Al Boum Photo** wasn't disgraced in first-time cheekpieces, having his first serious contest since last April, the joint-oldest in this field and likely to have to settle for just the 2 wins in this race; in touch, effort 3 out, chased leader briefly early in straight, no extra after 2 out. **Asterion Forlonge** ran respectably, keeping mistakes to a minimum after a hairy jump early on, making the running making sense in a race with little obvious pace, perhaps just stretched by the longer trip late on; led, mistake third, headed seventh, not fluent fourteenth, led again next, headed 3 out, no extra after 2 out. **Santini** wasn't disgraced, faring best of those that had contested the Cotswold Chase, just not the force he was when second to Al Boum Photo in the 2020 running; chased leaders, ridden fifteenth, weakened 3 out. **Aye Right** was well held, just not up to this class; pressed leader, jumped on seventh, headed fifteenth, weakened eighteenth; he's not in the Nationals coming up, which might have been a rather more realistic aim. **Tornado Flyer** had run with credit without getting fully competitive in Grade 1 chases at the Festival for the last 2 seasons and came here off a career best, but he ran no sort of race, his jumping going to pieces after he belted the first; soon behind, jumped poorly, labouring eighteenth, pulled up before 2 out. **Chantry House** again in cheekpieces, was hard to fancy on the way that he had won the Cotswold, but this was still a second stinker in 3 starts, even more dismal than his run in the King George, serious concerns about his attitude and jumping now, despite his seemingly impressive form figures (as opposed to form); in rear, jumped sketchily, never travelling well, pulled up before eighteenth.

TIMEFORM'S BEST OF 2021/22

For the second year running Henry de Bromhead completed the Champion Hurdle-Gold Cup double, though unlike the year before it was a double shared this time by Rachel Blackmore. Honeysuckle retained her crown in the Champion Hurdle, while in the Gold Cup A Plus Tard went one better than the year before, making Blackmore the first jockey to win both races at the same Festival since Sir Anthony McCoy in 1997. Otherwise, though, it was Willie Mullins who dominated at the Festival, not for the first time, of course, but his total of 10 winners, including a five-timer on Gold Cup day, set a new record, though top novice chaser Galopin des Champs really should have made it 11. Among those wins was an overdue first success, thanks to Energumene, for Mullins in what was a dramatic edition of the Queen Mother Champion Chase after chief rival Shishkin was pulled up. The latter had emerged just the best after the two best chasers in training had first clashed in the Clarence House Chase at Ascot, a candidate for race of the season. Mullins also won the King George VI Chase at Kempton with outsider Tornado Flyer, while at home he won his sixteenth Irish trainers' championship, with Energumene and Allaho, who'd won his second Ryanair Chase at Cheltenham, featuring among the stable's nine Grade 1 winners at the Punchestown Festival. There was also Irish success in the Grand National with novice Noble Yeats, trained by Emmet Mullins, Willie's nephew, springing a surprise under leading British amateur Sam Waley-Cohen, who announced his retirement afterwards. Shishkin's trainer Nicky Henderson has a new star to look forward to in the hurdling ranks with Constitution Hill, who looks a big threat to Honeysuckle's unbeaten record after putting up an outstanding performance to win the Supreme Novices' Hurdle at Cheltenham. However, it was Paul Nicholls who claimed his thirteenth British trainers' championship, ending the season with a five-timer on the final day at Sandown. Brian Hughes regained his champion jockey title, becoming only the fourth jockey after Peter Scudamore, Sir Anthony McCoy and Richard Johnson to ride 200 winners in a season. Paul Townend was Ireland's champion jockey again and was leading rider at the Cheltenham Festival with five winners.

Staying chasers

Henry de Bromhead once again saddled the first two in the Cheltenham Gold Cup, but the principals from 2021 finished the other way round this time and **A Plus Tard** (c178) was a much more decisive winner than **Minella Indo** (c165+) had been when beating him the year before, storming up the run-in to a 15-length success while his stablemate finished rather tamely. Although placed earlier in the season in the Champion Chase at Down Royal and the Irish Gold Cup at Leopardstown, Minella Indo has struggled for consistency since his Gold Cup victory, whereas A Plus Tard proved better than ever, not just at Cheltenham but also when beating an admittedly mixed bag of rivals by a still wider margin, 22 lengths, in the Betfair Chase at Haydock. Between then and the Gold Cup, A Plus Tard suffered an odds-on reverse in the Savills Chase at Leopardstown where **Galvin** (c164) dug deep into his stamina reserves to get the verdict by a short head. That was Galvin's seventh win from his last eight starts (**Frodon** (c163) beat him in the Champion Chase at Down Royal), but

A Plus Tard begins to pull clear of Minella Indo in the Gold Cup

subsequent events showed that result flattered him somewhat as he could finish only a remote fourth behind A Plus Tard at Cheltenham. Aintree's Many Clouds Chase winner **Protektorat** (c164), only a seven-year-old, fared best of the British to take third in the Gold Cup but found Aintree coming too soon afterwards. After his customary successful return at Tramore on New Year's Day, **Al Boum Photo** (c166) could finish only sixth in cheekpieces in another bid to win his third Cheltenham Gold Cup and, while he was back to his best when third in the Punchestown Gold Cup next time, just ahead of stablemate **Kemboy** (c166x), he was retired after being pulled up in the Grand Steeple-Chase de Paris at Auteuil. They were among five runners for Willie Mullins in a terrific renewal of the Punchestown Gold Cup which was won by their stablemate **Allaho** (c179) with a performance that, at the very least, matched A Plus Tard's effort at Cheltenham. Allaho was typically unrelenting from the front, though broke new ground in winning for the first time over three miles over fences which could open up more opportunities for him this season. He came home 14 lengths clear of the previous year's winner **Clan des Obeaux** (c168), who had returned to form in a change of headgear (blinkers replacing cheekpieces) to win the Bowl Chase at Aintree for the second year running on his previous start. Allaho had won all three of his races at around two and a half miles earlier in the campaign, notably the John Durkan Memorial Punchestown Chase and when giving a repeat performance of his impressive display the year before in the Ryanair Chase at Cheltenham. **Fakir d'Oudairies** (c166) finished behind Allaho on three occasions in Ireland but, as well as winning the Melling Chase at Aintree for the second year, he gained another Grade 1 success in Britain beforehand in the Ascot

Chase. The King George VI Chase also went to Ireland as **Tornado Flyer** (c163) ran the race of his life to beat former dual winner Clan des Obeaux, while an outsider also won the Irish Gold Cup at Leopardstown in the shape of **Conflated** (c166), later a faller in the Ryanair and runner-up in the Bowl at Aintree. Also worth noting was a top-class effort from Bobbyjo Chase winner **Any Second Now** (c166), who went one better than the year before when runner-up under a big weight in the Grand National.

Two-mile chasers

Both unbeaten as novices the previous season, **Shishkin** (c181) and **Energumene** (c180) proved outstanding recruits to the two-mile chasing scene for Nicky Henderson and Willie Mullins respectively. The latter had missed the Arkle, won by Shishkin, in 2020/21 but the pair clashed twice last season with very different results. Having won the Desert Orchid Chase on his return at Kempton, Shishkin made it 10 wins in a row when getting the better of Energumene by a length in a tremendous Clarence House Chase at Ascot after the runner-up, who'd gone with zest from the front and was still two lengths up at the last, was only worn down close home. The rematch in the Queen Mother Champion Chase at Cheltenham proved a big let-down, however, with Shishkin struggling from the word go and pulled up after the eighth while Energumene, patiently ridden this time, landed the spoils. Shishkin's connections initially blamed the softening ground on a thoroughly wet second day of the Festival, but a rare bone condition later came to light which ruled Shishkin out for the rest of the season. Meanwhile, Energumene, who'd won the Hilly Way

Energumene (right) leads Shishkin over the last at Ascot

Chase at Cork prior to Ascot, put up another top-notch performance to beat top-class stablemate and previous year's winner **Chacun Pour Soi** (c174) in the Champion Chase at Punchestown. The latter added to the drama in the Queen Mother Champion Chase when unseating at Cheltenham in what was a rare jumping lapse, but he'd been faultless in that department when winning the Dublin Chase at Leopardstown for the third year running. This trio were much the best in the two-mile division. **Greaneteen** (c166) took advantage of Shishkin's delayed return, and an out-of-sorts Chacun Pour Soi, to win the Tingle Creek Chase at Sandown and returned there to win the Celebration Chase at the end of the season. In between he was no match for Shishkin at Kempton and ran poorly in the Dublin Chase. Like the Shloer Chase winner **Nube Negra** (c164), Greaneteen was missing from the Queen Mother Champion Chase field in which 40/1 shot **Funambule Sivola** (c162), winner of the Game Spirit Chase at Newbury beforehand, took the runner-up spot behind Energumene. The 2021 Clarence House winner **First Flow** (c163) was no match for the big two in the latest renewal, though had earlier beaten Funambule Sivola when stepped up in trip for the Peterborough Chase at Huntingdon. Former star novice **Envoi Allen** (c161) had his limitations exposed, at least over two miles (he looks well worth another try over further), not fully convincing in beating two rivals in the Paddy's Rewards Club Chase at Leopardstown before finishing third in the Champion Chases at both Cheltenham and Punchestown.

Novice chasers

Mullins had another strong crop of novice chasers with no more exciting prospect among them than **Galopin des Champs** (c175p). He was unlucky not to be unbeaten, looking to have the Turners' Novices Chase at Cheltenham in safe keeping when coming down at the last and handing victory to **Bob Olinger** (c161?). Galopin des Champs was hard to fault otherwise, impressing with Grade 1 victories at Leopardstown and Fairyhouse either side of Cheltenham with **Master McShee** (c159), a Grade 1 winner at Limerick himself in December, chasing him home both times. Raced only at around two and a half miles over fences, Galopin des Champs could go up or down in trip, but he's already on the verge of being Gold Cup standard. Former Ballymore winner Bob Olinger's campaign began very promisingly but unraveled quickly, unimpressive when gifted the race at Cheltenham and looking a horse with problems when pulled up at Punchestown. **Ferny Hollow** (c166+) and **Gentleman de Mee** (c164p) were Mullins' other top novices, though Ferny Hollow had another interrupted season which ended in December with victory in the Racing Post Novice Chase at Leopardstown. Gentleman de Mee won his last three starts, culminating with upsetting the odds-on **Edwardstone** (c161) in the Maghull Novices' Chase at Aintree. The likeable Edwardstone was the top two-mile novice in Britain, winning his five other completed outings, notably the Henry VIII Novices' Chase at Sandown and the Sporting Life Arkle at Cheltenham where he had another Mullins novice, **Blue Lord** (c158), back in third. That was Blue Lord's only defeat in five chases when proving a bit too keen and came between Grade 1 wins in the Irish Arkle at Leopardstown and the Barberstown Castle Novice Chase at Punchestown. Over longer trips, there was little to choose between three of the best novices in Britain with **L'Homme Presse** (c162p) rated marginally the best of them. He progressed to win his first five chases, culminating in victory in the Brown Advisory Novices' Chase at Cheltenham when stepping up to three miles for the first time to beat **Ahoy Senor** (c161p). It was a different story when the pair met again on less testing ground in the Mildmay Novices' Chase at Aintree where Ahoy Senor jumped better than at Cheltenham and ran out a convincing winner from **Fury Road** (c156, a Grade 1 winner at Leopardstown in December) and a below-par L'Homme Presse. However, it was the fourth runner in the Mildmay, **Bravemansgame** (c159), who was sent off favourite having been pulled out at Cheltenham when the ground turned soft. He clearly wasn't himself when last at Aintree but had been unbeaten in four starts over fences beforehand, notably when showing too much speed for Ahoy Senor in the Kauto Star Novices' Chase at Kempton. **Stattler** (c160p), another for Mullins, won all three of his chases, notably the National Hunt Chase at Cheltenham, while the novice ranks also included Grand National winner **Noble Yeats** (c156), the first seven-year-old to win the race since 1940 and who'd earlier finished runner-up to Ahoy Senor in the Towton Novices' Chase at Wetherby.

Staying hurdlers

Flooring Porter (h162) joined some illustrious names to have won the Stayers' Hurdle at Cheltenham more than once and, while he's no Big Buck's, Flooring Porter impressed with some slick jumping in front as he was able to secure even more of an uncontested lead than he had when successful the year before. However, a bunched finish with some outsiders finishing close up prompts a cautious view of the form. **Klassical Dream** (h161) was only fifth in the Stayers' Hurdle but can be regarded as Flooring Porter's chief rival in the staying division and was sent off favourite at Cheltenham having beaten him for a second time in the Christmas Hurdle at Leopardstown. Unlike in their first meeting at the 2021 Punchestown Festival, Flooring Porter was on-song this time but Klassical Dream, who pinched a good lead early on, kept up a strong gallop to beat him by two lengths with the pair pulling a long way clear. Klassical Dream met with a surprise defeat in the Galmoy Hurdle at Gowran before Cheltenham where it was his turn to miss the break, but he went on to win a second Champion Stayers Hurdle at Punchestown (Flooring Porter absent) and then finish a good second in the Grande Course de Haies d'Auteuil. Old rivals **Thyme Hill** (h158) and **Paisley Park** (h158) were involved in a tight finish for the places in the Stayers' Hurdle, neither having been that well placed, and had earlier filled the same places behind **Champ** (h157) in the Long Walk Hurdle at Ascot. Returning from fences, Champ looked like becoming the new top staying hurdler at Ascot but met with an odds-on defeat to Paisley Park in the Cleeve Hurdle at Cheltenham next time (Paisley Park's third win in that contest) and then raced too freely when fourth in the Stayers' Hurdle and took only a remote third in the Liverpool Hurdle at Aintree in which **Sire du Berlais** (h159) inflicted a surprise defeat on Flooring Porter. Sire du Berlais had been badly hampered at Cheltenham when bidding for a third win in the Pertemps Final, but his Gordon Elliott stablemate **Commander of Fleet** (h158$) had better luck in the Coral Cup, pulling off a 50/1 shock in deteriorating conditions. The unreliable Commander of Fleet was better than ever at Cheltenham and that was his second long-priced win of the season in a valuable handicap after an earlier success at Navan. **Thomas Darby** (h152$) isn't one to trust either, but he came good in the

Honeysuckle is now unbeaten in 16 starts under Rules

Long Distance Hurdle at Newbury which was run to suit him and he showed similar form, despite finishing with less conviction, when fourth in the Long Walk.

Two-mile hurdlers

It might prove a different story in the coming months (see the novice hurdlers below), but the unbeaten reign of **Honeysuckle** (h165) as the dominant two-mile hurdler lasted for another season and never looked under much threat. In a carbon copy of her previous campaign, she again won the Hatton's Grace Hurdle at Fairyhouse and Irish Champion Hurdle at Leopardstown, both for a third time, before retaining her Champion Hurdle title at Cheltenham and then recording another straightforward success in the Punchestown Champion Hurdle which took her unbeaten record to 16 races. The only horse seriously backed against Honeysuckle all season in what remained a weak division was the previous year's runaway Supreme Novices' Hurdle winner **Appreciate It** (h160). A setback put his switch to fences on hold and he could finish only seventh in the Champion Hurdle after a whole year's absence. Instead, it was the 2020 winner **Epatante** (h156), third the year before, who followed Honeysuckle home in the Champion Hurdle. Epatante enjoyed a more rewarding campaign than the previous one otherwise, dead-heating with **Not So Sleepy** (h155) to win the Fighting Fifth Hurdle at Newcastle again, going one better than the year before when beating subsequent Betfair Hurdle winner/Champion Hurdle fifth **Glory And Fortune** (h153) in the Christmas Hurdle at Kempton and then stepping up in trip after the Champion Hurdle to win the Aintree Hurdle in clear-cut fashion. After some hard races, Epatante could be forgiven an odds-on defeat at Punchestown where she finished third behind stablemate **Marie's Rock** (h147) in the Mares Champion Hurdle. Runner-up in the two previous Champion Hurdles, **Sharjah** (h164) wasn't seen out after the turn of the year but added two more Grade 1 wins to his record before then, winning a second Morgiana Hurdle at Punchestown and a fourth successive Matheson Hurdle at Leopardstown. Runner-up in both those races was **Zanahiyr** (h160) whose only win came in the Grade 2 WKD Hurdle at Down Royal but who picked up more place money behind Honeysuckle at Leopardstown and Cheltenham and would have been second to Epatante at Aintree but for falling heavily at the last. Former County Hurdle winner **Saint Roi** (h155) ran up to his best when a never-dangerous fourth in the Champion Hurdle having previously finished third in the Matheson and fourth in the Irish Champion Hurdle. **Goshen** (h157) looked as good as ever when winning the Kingwell Hurdle at Wincanton for the second year running, following up a win in the Contenders Hurdle at Sandown, but he wasn't entered for the Champion Hurdle after hanging badly in the race the year before. **Tommy's Oscar** (h153) was one of the stories of the season, running up a four-timer in the North for Ann Hamilton's small yard and graduating from handicaps to win the Champion Hurdle Trial at Haydock, but he finished well held in the Champion Hurdle itself. **Sceau Royal** (h155) had his attentions switched back to fences later in the season but had earlier won the Elite Hurdle at Wincanton for a third time before finishing third in the Fighting Fifth.

Novice hurdlers

Not only was **Constitution Hill** (h177p) the standout novice over hurdles, but his rating made him much the best hurdler of the season full stop and as good as any novice hurdler in Timeform's experience in fact. He looked a novice of rare promise in making light of testing conditions in his first two starts at Sandown, including the Tolworth Novices' Hurdle, but a strongly-run race on better ground at Cheltenham allowed him to produce a breathtaking performance in the Supreme Novices' Hurdle in which he showed a fine turn of foot to pull 22 lengths clear of stable companion **Jonbon** (h153p). Jonbon began the season with a big reputation himself for Nicky Henderson and won all four of his other starts, notably when battling to a neck success after Cheltenham in the Top Novices' Hurdle at Aintree from one of Willie Mullins' best novices **El Fabiolo** (h152), who went on to win at Punchestown. Both of those are exciting novice chase prospects as is Mullins' Ballymore Novices' Hurdle winner **Sir Gerhard** (h152), a Grade 1 winner at the Dublin Racing Festival beforehand whose subsequent defeat in the two-mile Champion Novice Hurdle at Punchestown won by **Mighty Potter** (h148) shouldn't be held against him. Mighty Potter was pulled up in the Supreme but took his second Grade 1 of the season at Punchestown after beating **Three Stripe Life** (h147) for a Gordon Elliott one-two in the Future Champions Novice Hurdle at Leopardstown in December. Three Stripe Life was runner-up to Sir Gerhard on his next two starts before going one better in the Mersey Novices' Hurdle at Aintree, but he then came up short behind **State Man** (h155p) and dual Grade 2 winner **Flame Bearer** (h148) in the two-and-a-half-mile Champion Novice Hurdle at Punchestown. State Man stepped up in trip after winning the County Hurdle at Cheltenham from fellow novice **First Street** (h145) but is likely to be targeted by Mullins at the Champion Hurdle and looks the best prospect among the novices bar Constitution Hill. **Dysart Diamond** (h147) looked very promising, so much so he started joint-favourite for the Supreme when still unbeaten, but fell there and then ran poorly at Punchestown. Mullins also had the leading staying novice **The Nice Guy** (h150p) whose unbeaten record included the double of the Albert Bartlett Novices' Hurdle at Cheltenham and the Irish Mirror Novice Hurdle at Punchestown, with stablemate **Minella Cocooner** (h149), who'd been a Grade 1 winner himself at the Dublin Racing Festival, runner-up both times. **Hillcrest** (h144) was pulled up after starting favourite for the Albert Bartlett but won his other completed starts and looks very much the type to take to fences. Meanwhile, **Vauban** (h150P) looked a very exciting juvenile hurdler for Mullins in completing a Grade 1 hat-trick in the Spring Juvenile Hurdle at Leopardstown, the Triumph Hurdle at Cheltenham and the Champion Four Year Old Hurdle at Punchestown, with **Fil Dor** (h144) chasing him home each time.

HORSES TO FOLLOW
2021/22 STATISTICS (Britain)

TRAINERS (1,2,3 earnings)	Horses	Indiv'l Wnrs	Races Won	Runs	% Strike Rate	Stakes £
1 Paul Nicholls	184	89	143	629	22.7	2,836,471
2 Nicky Henderson	171	77	120	561	21.4	2,387,238
3 Dan Skelton	211	95	135	742	18.2	1,974,681
4 W. P. Mullins, Ireland	78	15	15	89	16.9	1,612,511
5 Venetia Williams	83	34	60	292	20.5	1,473,964
6 Nigel Twiston-Davies	116	46	68	468	14.5	1,312,277
7 Fergal O'Brien	200	78	128	739	17.3	1,297,118
8 Donald McCain	139	73	155	663	23.4	1,281,713
9 Alan King	122	42	63	435	14.5	1,255,684
10 Gary Moore	109	57	91	440	20.7	1,117,812

JOCKEYS (by winners)	1st	2nd	3rd	Unpl	Total Rides	% Strike Rate
1 Brian Hughes	204	161	147	444	956	21.3
2 Sam Twiston-Davies	105	123	78	425	731	14.4
3 Harry Skelton	103	84	76	245	508	20.3
4 Harry Cobden	99	78	61	189	427	23.2
5 Sean Bowen	95	62	71	263	491	19.3
6 Paddy Brennan	87	77	63	182	409	21.3
7 Jamie Moore	80	61	51	224	416	19.2
8 Sean Quinlan	78	84	88	383	633	12.3
9 James Bowen	74	64	52	198	388	19.1
10 Nico de Boinville	74	43	31	204	352	21.0

SIRES OF WINNERS (1,2,3 earnings)	Races Won	Runs	% Strike Rate	Stakes £
1 Yeats (by Sadler's Wells)	117	724	16.2	2,032,768
2 Fame And Glory (by Montjeu)	118	717	16.5	1,499,542
3 Kapgarde (by Garde Royale)	56	311	18.0	1,454,688
4 Midnight Legend (by Night Shift)	81	534	15.2	1,289,837
5 Getaway (by Monsun)	110	959	11.5	1,196,554
6 Milan (by Sadler's Wells)	91	661	13.8	1,156,506
7 Kayf Tara (by Sadler's Wells)	73	578	12.6	1,090,209
8 Flemensfirth (by Alleged)	65	506	12.8	983,631
9 Stowaway (by Slip Anchor)	53	430	12.3	918,651
10 Mahler (by Galileo)	90	554	16.2	911,644

LEADING HORSES (1,2,3 earnings)	Races Won	Runs	Stakes £
1 Noble Yeats 6 b.g Yeats - That'S Moyne	1	3	509,616
2 A Plus Tard 7 b.g Kapgarde - Turboka	2	2	474,208
3 Epatante 7 b.m No Risk At All - Kadjara	3	4	369,897
4 Energumene 7 br.g Denham Red - Olinight	1	2	266,455
5 Honeysuckle 7 b.m Sulamani - First Royal	1	1	253,215
6 Edwardstone 7 b.g Kayf Tara - Nothingtoloose	5	7	247,014
7 Flooring Porter 6 b.g Yeats - Lillymile	1	2	235,653
8 Fakir D'Oudairies 6 b.g Kapgarde - Niagaria Du Bois	2	2	233,430
9 L'Homme Presse 6 b.g Diamond Boy - Romance Turgot	5	6	222,014
10 Allaho 7 b.g No Risk At All - Idaho Falls	1	1	214,762

SECTION

5

HORSES TO FOLLOW

THE TIMEFORM TOP 100

Hurdlers

Rating	Horse
177p	Constitution Hill
165	Honeysuckle
164	Sharjah
162	Flooring Porter
161	Klassical Dream
160	Appreciate It
160	Zanahiyr
159	Buzz
159	Sire du Berlais
158	Aspire Tower
158	Paisley Park
158	Thyme Hill
158§	Commander of Fleet
157	Abacadabras
157	Champ
157	Goshen
157	Jason The Militant
156	Epatante
155p	State Man
155	Not So Sleepy
155	Saint Roi
155	Sceau Royal
155	Sporting John
155	The Storyteller
155	Thedevilscoachman
154	Mcfabulous
154	Silver Streak
154	Teahupoo
153p	Jonbon
153	Adagio
153	Ashdale Bob
153	Brewin'upastorm
153	Darasso
153	Glory And Fortune
153	Tommy's Oscar
152	El Fabiolo
152	James du Berlais
152	Sir Gerhard
152	Sole Pretender
152§	Thomas Darby
151+	Saldier
151	Concertista
151	Home By The Lee
151	Koshari

Rating	Horse
150P	Vauban
150p	The Nice Guy
150	Buveur d'Air
150	Darver Star
150	Echoes In Rain
150	Gentlemansgame
150	Milkwood
149	Beauport
149	Dashel Drasher
149	Fastorslow
149	Minella Cocooner
149	Summerville Boy
148	Bacardys
148	Call Me Lyreen
148	Eskylane
148	Flame Bearer
148	Magic Tricks
148	Mighty Potter
148	Quilixios
148	Sams Profile
148	Soaring Glory
147	Allmankind
147	Ballyandy
147	Cilaos Emery
147	Dysart Dynamo
147	Guard Your Dreams
147	Marie's Rock
147	Monmiral
147	Royal Kahala
147	Third Wind
147	Three Stripe Life
147	Vanillier
146	Arcadian Sunrise
146	Bapaume
146	Cash Back
146	Elixir de Nutz
146	Journey With Me
146	Langer Dan
146	Proschema
146	Scaramanga
146	Stormy Ireland
146	Telmesomethinggirl
146	Tritonic
146?	Zurekin
145p	Blazing Khal
145	Adrien du Pont

Rating	Horse
145	Andy Dufresne
145	Botox Has
145	Brinkley
145	Camprond
145	Diego du Charmil
145	Fils d'Oudairies
145	First Street
145	Fusil Raffles
145	Ginto
145	Grand Roi
145	Indefatigable
145	Jury Duty
145	Minella Drama
145	North Lodge
145	Queens Brook
145	Saint Felicien
145	The Shunter
145x	Hang In There

Chasers

Rating	Horse
181	Shishkin
180	Energumene
179	Allaho
178	A Plus Tard
175p	Galopin des Champs
174	Chacun Pour Soi
168	Clan des Obeaux
167	Monkfish
166+	Ferny Hollow
166	Al Boum Photo
166	Any Second Now
166	Conflated
166	Fakir d'Oudairies
166	Greaneteen
165+	Minella Indo
165x	Kemboy
164p	Gentleman de Mee
164	Galvin
164	Nube Negra
164	Protektorat
163	Easy Game
163	Eldorado Allen
163	First Flow
163	Frodon
163	Royal Rendezvous

Rating	Horse
163	Saint Calvados
163	Tornado Flyer
162p	L'Homme Presse
162	Andy Dufresne
162	Funambule Sivola
162	Janidil
162	Mister Fisher
162	Royale Pagaille
162x	Asterion Forlonge
161p	Ahoy Senor
161	Chris's Dream
161	Edwardstone
161	Envoi Allen
161	The Storyteller
161?	Bob Olinger
160p	Stattler
160+	Champ
160	Bristol de Mai
160	Capodanno
160	Delta Work
160	Dunvegan
160	Hitman
160	Two For Gold
160§	Chantry House
159	Blackbow
159	Bravemansgame
159	Captain Guinness
159	Dashel Drasher
159	Farouk d'Alene
159	Hewick
159	Master McShee
159	Melon
159	Sceau Royal
159	Shan Blue
158	Blue Lord
158	Colreevy
158	Fanion d'Estruval
158	Franco de Port
158?	Allmankind
157	Fiddlerontheroof
157x	Master Tommytucker
156+	Gaillard du Mesnil
156	Aye Right
156	Cepage
156	Coeur Sublime
156	Eklat de Rire

156	Fury Road	134	Icare Allen
156	Noble Yeats	134	Iceo
156	Paint The Dream	134	The Tide Turns
156	Politologue	132p	Gaelic Warrior
156	Yala Enki	132	Prairie Dancer
155	Bapaume	131p	Bell Ex One
155	Burrows Saint	131+	Hms Seahorse
155	Editeur du Gite	131+	Iberique du Seuil
155	Escaria Ten	129	Doctor Parnassus
155	Gabynako	129	Lunar Power
155	Longhouse Poet	129	Teddy Blue
155	Lostintranslation	128P	In This World
155	Midnight Shadow	128+	Man O Work
155	Sam Brown	128	Impulsive One
155x	Beacon Edge	127p	Saint Segal
154	Acapella Bourgeois	127	Ebasari
154	Chosen Mate	127	Graystone
154	Early Doors	126	Iroko
154	Imperial Alcazar	125	Ben Siegel
154	Lifetime Ambition	125	Faron
154	Nuts Well	125	Message Personnel
154	Run Wild Fred	125	Skycutter
154	Simply The Betts	125	Un des Flos
154	The Shunter	125	Hudson de Grugy
154	Tiger Roll	124p	Samarrive
154	Win My Wings	124	Elham Valley
153p	Jungle Boogie	124	Homme Public
153p	Pencilfulloflead	124	Sage Advice
153+	Ballyoisin	124	Tinnahalla
153	Chatham Street Lad		
153	Darasso		
153	El Barra		
153	Pic d'Orhy		
153	Ronald Pump		
153x	Brahma Bull		
153x	Cilaos Emery		
153?	Espoir de Romay		
153?	Minella Times		

Juvenile Hurdlers

150P	Vauban
144	Fil Dor
141	Brazil
141	Knight Salute
141	Pied Piper
138	Il Etait Temps
136	Britzka
135	Petit Tonnerre
135	Porticello

Novice Hurdlers

177p	Constitution Hill
155p	State Man
153p	Jonbon
152	El Fabiolo
152	Sir Gerhard
150p	The Nice Guy
149	Minella Cocooner
148	Flame Bearer
148	Mighty Potter
147	Dysart Dynamo
147	Three Stripe Life
146	Journey With Me
145p	Blazing Khal
145	First Street
145	Ginto
145	North Lodge
144	Hillcrest
144	Kilcruit

144	Meet And Greet
144	Minella Crooner
143p	Gelino Bello
143	I Like To Move It
143	Suprise Package
142p	Party Central
142	Farout
142	Might I
141	Classic Getaway
141	Colonel Mustard
141	Hallowed Star
141	Hollow Games
141	Jacksons Gold
140p	Pay The Piper
140	Calico
140	Faivoir
140	Metier
140	Shanroe
140	Telmesomethinggirl

Novice Chasers

175p	Galopin des Champs
166+	Ferny Hollow
164p	Gentleman de Mee
162p	L'Homme Presse
161p	Ahoy Senor
161	Edwardstone
161?	Bob Olinger
160p	Stattler
160	Capodanno
159	Bravemansgame
159	Farouk d'Alene
159	Hewick
159	Master McShee
158	Blue Lord
156+	Gaillard du Mesnil
156	Coeur Sublime
156	Fury Road
156	Noble Yeats
155	Gabynako
155x	Beacon Edge
154	Imperial Alcazar
154	Lifetime Ambition
154	Run Wild Fred
153p	Jungle Boogie
153	El Barra
153	Pic d'Orhy
152	Cape Gentleman
152	Ciel de Neige

152	Stolen Silver
152	Third Time Lucki

National Hunt Flat Horses

128	Facile Vega
126	Redemption Day
122	American Mike
118	James's Gate
117	Twinjets
116	Luccia
115	Lookaway
114	Seabank Bistro
113	Authorised Speed
113	Sergeant Wilson
112	Fame And Concrete
112	Hullnback
111+	Leave of Absence
111	Impulsive Dancer
111	The Big Doyen
110+	Mercurey
110	Ernest Gray
110	Rath Gaul Boy
110	Sandor Clegane
110	Top Dog
109	Ashroe Diamond
109	Itswhatunitesus
108p	Springwell Bay
107+	Henri The Second
107	Blue Beach
107	Densworth
107	Pembroke
107	Western Zephyr
106	Are U Wise To That
106	Ballyglass
106	Blow Your Wad
106	I Am Fortunata
106	The Mediator
106	Timeforatune
106	Luttrell Lad
106	Party Central
106	Rainyday Woman
106	Ramilles

TRAINERS FOR COURSES

The following statistics show the most successful trainers over the past five seasons at each of the courses that stage National Hunt racing in England, Scotland and Wales. Impact Value is expressed as a factor of a trainer's number of winners compared to those expected to occur by chance. Market Value is expressed as the factor by which the % chance of an Industry Starting Price exceeds random, as implied by field size. For example, a horse that is shorter than 3/1 in a 4-runner field will have a Market Value above 1.

AINTREE

Trainer	Wins	Runs	Strike Rate	% Rivals Beaten	P/L	Run To Form %	Impact Value	Market Value
Dan Skelton	24	152	15.79%	59.74	48.55	65.79	1.43	1.52
Nicky Henderson	19	117	16.24%	52.27	-55.01	54.27	1.69	1.82
Paul Nicholls	15	111	13.51%	50.58	-23.47	50.45	1.40	1.71
Gordon Elliott, Ireland	7	51	13.73%	59.98	6.50	57.84	2.24	1.97
Alan King	7	49	14.29%	60.70	2.88	67.35	1.59	1.62
Nigel Twiston-Davies	7	78	8.97%	47.25	-44.50	47.44	0.98	1.43
W. P. Mullins, Ireland	6	38	15.79%	58.23	-6.50	59.21	2.19	2.13
Peter Bowen	6	38	15.79%	52.64	11.50	56.58	1.54	0.96
Olly Murphy	6	45	13.33%	57.26	-9.67	64.44	1.20	1.47
Harry Fry	6	43	13.95%	57.57	-9.27	66.28	1.27	1.26

ASCOT

Trainer	Wins	Runs	Strike Rate	% Rivals Beaten	P/L	Run To Form %	Impact Value	Market Value
Nicky Henderson	33	156	21.15%	59.94	0.20	70.51	1.56	1.85
Paul Nicholls	30	188	15.96%	52.03	-14.95	61.44	1.17	1.47
Dan Skelton	16	97	16.49%	52.02	15.66	57.22	1.32	1.02
Gary Moore	11	108	10.19%	46.82	-42.85	46.76	0.89	1.04
Venetia Williams	9	55	16.36%	52.68	-8.45	56.36	1.36	1.29
Nigel Twiston-Davies	9	78	11.54%	49.53	-16.75	53.85	0.95	1.16
Harry Fry	9	51	17.65%	57.62	-10.70	64.71	1.63	1.49
Dr Richard Newland	7	43	16.28%	57.84	13.25	65.12	1.38	1.26
Kim Bailey	7	45	15.56%	56.53	-10.26	67.78	1.20	1.50
Alan King	6	70	8.57%	51.84	-36.27	60.00	0.79	1.28

AYR

Trainer	Wins	Runs	Strike Rate	% Rivals Beaten	P/L	Run To Form %	Impact Value	Market Value
Nicky Richards	36	180	20.00%	63.45	-41.54	66.11	1.62	1.88
N. W. Alexander	30	220	13.64%	54.40	33.25	57.05	1.17	1.02
Lucinda Russell	28	236	11.86%	54.91	-45.82	60.59	0.94	1.10
Sandy Thomson	16	109	14.68%	55.34	-45.68	60.09	1.13	1.50
Donald McCain	14	62	22.58%	48.91	-10.56	59.68	1.46	1.39
Dan Skelton	12	46	26.09%	73.59	-1.12	76.09	2.26	1.78
Stuart Crawford, Ireland	12	93	12.90%	48.80	-33.06	55.38	1.05	1.32
Rose Dobbin	11	64	17.19%	51.90	-16.63	45.31	1.43	1.13
Iain Jardine	11	85	12.94%	51.48	-27.49	50.59	1.12	1.12
Gordon Elliott, Ireland	11	49	22.45%	66.16	-14.49	72.45	1.67	2.15

BANGOR-ON-DEE

Trainer	Wins	Runs	Strike Rate	% Rivals Beaten	P/L	Run To Form %	Impact Value	Market Value
Donald McCain	66	303	21.78%	62.89	30.39	65.02	1.72	1.52
Dan Skelton	22	122	18.03%	53.68	-42.99	54.92	1.49	1.99
Jennie Candlish	14	88	15.91%	57.87	-8.24	54.55	1.34	1.14
Olly Murphy	13	79	16.46%	51.48	-39.24	52.53	1.32	1.63
Alan King	13	55	23.64%	66.10	-8.14	66.36	1.68	2.26
Jonjo O'Neill	11	73	15.07%	53.03	-19.83	58.90	1.32	1.26
Alastair Ralph	11	62	17.74%	54.32	78.50	54.84	1.38	1.09
Gary Hanmer	11	74	14.86%	49.81	-16.08	47.30	1.14	0.97
Henry Daly	11	45	24.44%	63.25	33.75	60.00	2.04	1.08
Fergal O'Brien	11	50	22.00%	60.88	4.85	58.00	1.75	1.66

CARLISLE

Trainer	Wins	Runs	Strike Rate	% Rivals Beaten	P/L	Run To Form %	Impact Value	Market Value
Donald McCain	33	196	16.84%	58.71	-30.18	63.52	1.28	1.48
Nicky Richards	31	121	25.62%	61.41	54.50	64.88	1.86	1.45
Rose Dobbin	12	68	17.65%	49.29	2.83	53.68	1.43	1.18
Jonjo O'Neill	12	59	20.34%	55.44	51.97	56.78	1.71	1.61
Stuart Crawford, Ireland	11	52	21.15%	63.41	-7.21	64.42	1.58	1.56
Stuart Coltherd	11	73	15.07%	56.29	0.33	63.01	1.26	1.18
Lucinda Russell	11	135	8.15%	45.97	-9.25	44.81	0.68	0.97
Micky Hammond	11	123	8.94%	41.59	-18.23	39.43	0.73	0.83
Nigel Twiston-Davies	10	32	31.25%	65.17	4.75	68.75	2.56	2.52
Brian Ellison	9	61	14.75%	56.43	-9.49	59.84	1.19	1.45

CARTMEL

Trainer	Wins	Runs	Strike Rate	% Rivals Beaten	P/L	Run To Form %	Impact Value	Market Value
James Moffatt	27	202	13.37%	48.68	-26.99	43.32	1.05	1.12
Donald McCain	24	146	16.44%	58.51	-48.71	55.14	1.18	1.50
Peter Bowen	20	92	21.74%	56.02	24.34	58.15	1.56	1.55
Dianne Sayer	15	81	18.52%	54.09	-20.63	44.44	1.51	1.29
Sam England	9	47	19.15%	59.64	17.75	60.64	1.65	1.36
Martin Todhunter	8	39	20.51%	52.83	-8.13	50.00	1.66	1.50
Micky Hammond	6	94	6.38%	48.70	-58.38	45.74	0.54	0.99
Iain Jardine	6	28	21.43%	54.56	-5.75	60.71	1.67	1.46
Ben Haslam	6	32	18.75%	47.94	92.50	53.13	1.47	0.95
Jennie Candlish	6	37	16.22%	57.64	-8.75	55.41	1.37	1.37

CATTERICK BRIDGE

Trainer	Wins	Runs	Strike Rate	% Rivals Beaten	P/L	Run To Form %	Impact Value	Market Value
Donald McCain	24	148	16.22%	56.84	-26.16	60.14	1.27	1.61
Micky Hammond	14	179	7.82%	46.25	35.50	40.78	0.65	0.82
Sue Smith	13	86	15.12%	56.27	16.61	50.58	1.26	1.39
Sam England	11	63	17.46%	59.10	-8.09	61.11	1.33	1.42
Rebecca Menzies	10	48	20.83%	59.62	29.21	58.33	1.75	1.18
Jamie Snowden	9	19	47.37%	72.09	2.73	65.79	3.07	2.29
Philip Kirby	9	75	12.00%	50.67	4.21	52.00	1.09	0.83
Tim Easterby	7	56	12.50%	51.01	-3.50	51.79	1.17	0.85
Dan Skelton	7	37	18.92%	50.49	-18.96	56.76	1.55	2.40
Martin Keighley	6	29	20.69%	54.60	-7.12	56.90	1.50	1.31

CHELTENHAM

Trainer	Wins	Runs	Strike Rate	% Rivals Beaten	P/L	Run To Form %	Impact Value	Market Value
Nicky Henderson	45	306	14.71%	53.55	-45.80	59.80	1.60	1.72
W. P. Mullins, Ireland	35	301	11.63%	56.60	-28.11	67.61	1.58	1.82
Gordon Elliott, Ireland	29	221	13.12%	57.19	24.30	64.48	1.90	1.91
Fergal O'Brien	23	184	12.50%	56.53	6.92	65.76	1.34	1.43
Dan Skelton	23	246	9.35%	53.43	-84.24	62.40	0.92	1.28
Paul Nicholls	22	254	8.66%	51.57	-123.58	58.07	0.84	1.41
Nigel Twiston-Davies	22	233	9.44%	50.38	-70.32	54.08	0.92	1.17
Henry de Bromhead, Ireland	19	119	15.97%	52.72	28.03	61.34	1.69	1.38
David Pipe	10	108	9.26%	50.62	-43.54	54.63	1.13	1.20
Philip Hobbs	10	153	6.54%	50.23	-85.92	56.21	0.71	1.31

CHEPSTOW

Trainer	Wins	Runs	Strike Rate	% Rivals Beaten	P/L	Run To Form %	Impact Value	Market Value
Paul Nicholls	53	197	26.90%	66.75	-5.78	73.86	2.24	2.44
Evan Williams	31	249	12.45%	52.97	19.46	53.41	1.22	1.28
Philip Hobbs	21	144	14.58%	52.81	-6.33	52.43	1.38	1.56
David Pipe	17	102	16.67%	63.06	3.73	63.24	1.63	1.55
Tom Lacey	17	66	25.76%	62.48	36.25	61.36	2.34	1.52
Venetia Williams	16	126	12.70%	54.69	-40.72	54.76	1.18	1.47
Fergal O'Brien	14	113	12.39%	53.50	-53.36	56.64	1.05	1.53
Dan Skelton	14	120	11.67%	55.09	-8.18	54.17	1.06	1.39
Neil Mulholland	12	95	12.63%	50.67	1.08	46.84	1.38	1.01
Jonjo O'Neill	11	108	10.19%	54.83	-66.24	56.02	0.99	1.41

DONCASTER

Trainer	Wins	Runs	Strike Rate	% Rivals Beaten	P/L	Run To Form %	Impact Value	Market Value
Dan Skelton	23	116	19.83%	55.67	-10.52	59.48	1.43	1.46
Nicky Henderson	18	85	21.18%	58.98	-29.32	61.76	1.76	2.71
Paul Nicholls	16	74	21.62%	55.76	-22.47	60.81	1.34	1.58
Alan King	14	115	12.17%	54.50	-47.77	53.91	0.91	1.50
Ian Williams	12	75	16.00%	48.85	28.29	48.67	1.40	1.16
Charlie Longsdon	11	89	12.36%	48.72	-12.02	57.87	1.03	0.98
Ben Pauling	11	79	13.92%	47.64	40.13	44.94	1.13	1.11
Donald McCain	11	79	13.92%	53.97	4.33	51.27	1.07	1.21
Fergal O'Brien	10	52	19.23%	61.88	18.50	57.69	1.53	1.53
Nigel Twiston-Davies	10	58	17.24%	48.40	-2.54	49.14	1.33	1.18

EXETER

Trainer	Wins	Runs	Strike Rate	% Rivals Beaten	P/L	Run To Form %	Impact Value	Market Value
Philip Hobbs	31	223	13.90%	54.17	-81.67	59.19	1.16	1.67
Paul Nicholls	27	116	23.28%	64.16	-22.10	69.40	1.78	2.19
David Pipe	20	188	10.64%	49.09	-64.04	48.67	1.06	1.36
Harry Fry	20	76	26.32%	65.86	25.11	66.45	2.23	2.57
Evan Williams	19	104	18.27%	49.88	26.00	50.96	1.42	1.21
Susan Gardner	14	123	11.38%	48.38	-2.50	42.68	1.07	0.91
Anthony Honeyball	13	52	25.00%	58.72	3.18	55.77	2.21	2.20
Jeremy Scott	12	114	10.53%	58.26	-22.80	55.26	1.08	1.39
Venetia Williams	11	86	12.79%	53.54	-46.47	52.91	1.12	1.54
Fergal O'Brien	10	84	11.90%	57.32	-51.67	62.50	1.02	1.71

FAKENHAM

Trainer	Wins	Runs	Strike Rate	% Rivals Beaten	P/L	Run To Form %	Impact Value	Market Value
Olly Murphy	36	152	23.68%	59.51	-20.07	62.83	1.41	1.53
Lucy Wadham	23	77	29.87%	61.27	18.91	62.99	1.91	1.45
Christian Williams	18	62	29.03%	59.14	7.14	62.10	1.93	1.55
Stuart Edmunds	15	46	32.61%	62.91	49.42	63.04	2.06	1.47
Neil King	11	83	13.25%	45.37	-5.70	54.22	0.83	1.02
Dr Richard Newland	10	44	22.73%	61.09	-6.55	64.77	1.39	1.62
Nicky Henderson	9	34	26.47%	65.45	-12.77	69.12	1.59	2.46
Alan King	9	31	29.03%	58.29	10.77	56.45	1.74	1.67
Dan Skelton	8	43	18.60%	57.24	-13.73	56.98	1.13	1.38
Gary Moore	8	42	19.05%	53.83	-15.20	64.29	1.15	1.11

FFOS LAS

Trainer	Wins	Runs	Strike Rate	% Rivals Beaten	P/L	Run To Form %	Impact Value	Market Value
Evan Williams	44	313	14.06%	49.94	-34.54	48.40	1.10	1.13
Peter Bowen	36	229	15.72%	48.73	-31.20	46.07	1.24	1.21
David Rees	15	118	12.71%	51.65	8.13	41.95	1.12	1.14
David Pipe	15	89	16.85%	53.93	-24.78	57.30	1.39	1.61
Nigel Twiston-Davies	14	90	15.56%	55.55	-18.30	48.89	1.27	1.56
Tim Vaughan	13	142	9.15%	46.07	-28.63	42.96	0.76	0.95
Nicky Henderson	13	34	38.24%	65.32	1.63	64.71	2.40	2.38
Rebecca Curtis	11	71	15.49%	56.53	-5.00	56.34	1.26	1.32
Venetia Williams	11	52	21.15%	56.75	8.75	54.81	1.95	1.62
Neil Mulholland	11	87	12.64%	49.29	-2.38	52.87	1.03	1.01

FONTWELL PARK

Trainer	Wins	Runs	Strike Rate	% Rivals Beaten	P/L	Run To Form %	Impact Value	Market Value
Gary Moore	78	397	19.65%	55.67	-11.73	59.95	1.35	1.48
Chris Gordon	32	219	14.61%	55.40	-21.91	57.31	1.11	1.29
Anthony Honeyball	30	81	37.04%	70.06	35.46	72.84	2.55	2.20
Paul Nicholls	30	80	37.50%	71.90	-1.41	75.63	1.96	2.29
Neil Mulholland	28	195	14.36%	53.17	2.82	56.41	1.04	1.25
Jamie Snowden	20	89	22.47%	60.50	-12.76	61.80	1.47	1.37
Oliver Sherwood	17	87	19.54%	58.38	13.76	63.22	1.42	1.46
Olly Murphy	15	71	21.13%	58.17	-18.35	62.68	1.36	1.69
Seamus Mullins	15	172	8.72%	43.86	-82.71	47.67	0.63	0.94
Philip Hobbs	15	70	21.43%	57.22	-22.91	60.71	1.42	2.05

TRAINERS FOR COURSES

HAYDOCK PARK

Trainer	Wins	Runs	Strike Rate	% Rivals Beaten	P/L	Run To Form %	Impact Value	Market Value
Donald McCain	18	108	16.67%	52.16	-34.26	53.24	1.10	1.10
Sue Smith	16	88	18.18%	58.90	-4.75	58.52	1.36	1.26
Nigel Twiston-Davies	13	92	14.13%	51.39	-20.44	49.46	1.07	1.26
Nicky Henderson	12	46	26.09%	54.52	-5.22	59.78	1.69	1.63
Paul Nicholls	12	47	25.53%	55.02	-16.75	70.21	1.72	1.69
Venetia Williams	12	63	19.05%	56.90	70.53	61.11	1.36	1.57
Jamie Snowden	9	25	36.00%	64.15	14.21	70.00	2.30	1.42
Fergal O'Brien	7	37	18.92%	55.19	0.93	62.16	1.54	1.05
David Pipe	7	46	15.22%	56.00	9.08	53.26	1.39	1.51
Jonjo O'Neill	7	36	19.44%	56.92	-6.88	56.94	1.74	1.61

HEREFORD

Trainer	Wins	Runs	Strike Rate	% Rivals Beaten	P/L	Run To Form %	Impact Value	Market Value
Venetia Williams	19	88	21.59%	51.61	13.38	52.27	1.85	1.39
Dan Skelton	17	70	24.29%	61.10	-9.40	62.14	1.93	2.15
Tom Symonds	11	50	22.00%	60.75	39.58	51.00	2.13	1.22
Evan Williams	11	130	8.46%	45.71	-62.52	43.08	0.72	0.99
Jonjo O'Neill	11	41	26.83%	62.88	11.98	64.63	2.03	1.53
Kim Bailey	11	42	26.19%	66.98	5.43	69.05	2.29	1.97
Neil Mulholland	10	41	24.39%	60.36	12.42	64.63	2.15	1.48
Paul Nicholls	10	37	27.03%	60.95	-6.75	62.16	1.64	2.24
Nigel Twiston-Davies	9	46	19.57%	54.75	-12.38	57.61	1.57	1.57
Kerry Lee	9	56	16.07%	51.41	-16.72	57.14	1.28	1.44

HEXHAM

Trainer	Wins	Runs	Strike Rate	% Rivals Beaten	P/L	Run To Form %	Impact Value	Market Value
Lucinda Russell	30	240	12.50%	56.08	-30.38	57.71	1.06	1.29
Micky Hammond	21	227	9.25%	46.00	-75.32	40.97	0.85	0.93
Nicky Richards	15	59	25.42%	60.81	-12.10	63.56	2.19	2.28
Maurice Barnes	15	162	9.26%	47.14	-86.88	46.91	0.77	0.96
Stuart Coltherd	14	105	13.33%	52.82	22.33	49.05	1.22	1.16
Sue Smith	12	113	10.62%	53.26	87.00	54.42	0.96	1.16
Ben Haslam	12	69	17.39%	52.93	9.30	52.90	1.41	1.19
Mark Walford	12	67	17.91%	60.83	-10.02	58.21	1.63	1.52
Jennie Candlish	11	42	26.19%	66.57	-3.45	66.67	2.28	1.80
Philip Kirby	10	95	10.53%	43.06	-58.72	40.53	0.94	1.30

HUNTINGDON

Trainer	Wins	Runs	Strike Rate	% Rivals Beaten	P/L	Run To Form %	Impact Value	Market Value
Dan Skelton	28	154	18.18%	58.61	-43.63	56.49	1.55	2.06
Nicky Henderson	24	98	24.49%	65.19	-39.09	69.39	1.88	2.73
Fergal O'Brien	23	89	25.84%	62.00	46.38	66.85	2.25	1.99
Olly Murphy	20	87	22.99%	61.72	-24.58	64.94	1.95	1.65
Jonjo O'Neill	19	101	18.81%	55.93	40.99	53.96	1.84	1.66
Gary Moore	18	124	14.52%	54.02	-17.25	55.24	1.18	1.36
Kim Bailey	16	111	14.41%	55.75	-32.00	55.41	1.20	1.51
Ben Pauling	14	100	14.00%	51.32	-38.36	44.50	1.22	1.55
Charlie Longsdon	13	112	11.61%	47.16	-28.25	48.66	1.06	1.10
Alan King	12	88	13.64%	62.25	-6.88	63.64	1.20	1.77

KELSO

Trainer	Wins	Runs	Strike Rate	% Rivals Beaten	P/L	Run To Form %	Impact Value	Market Value
Lucinda Russell	29	277	10.47%	50.17	-100.39	50.18	0.81	1.01
Sandy Thomson	24	140	17.14%	56.27	-33.02	62.14	1.30	1.36
N. W. Alexander	24	200	12.00%	49.83	50.43	52.75	0.97	1.05
Donald McCain	22	137	16.06%	52.27	-47.07	54.74	1.15	1.59
Keith Dalgleish	21	108	19.44%	55.56	9.47	55.56	1.54	1.74
Rose Dobbin	16	129	12.40%	56.69	-44.29	56.20	1.07	1.40
Stuart Coltherd	14	94	14.89%	48.78	-7.13	53.72	1.18	0.97
Nicky Richards	13	109	11.93%	57.28	-28.57	60.55	0.93	1.84
Iain Jardine	12	78	15.38%	56.86	-10.20	52.56	1.32	1.33
James Ewart	11	78	14.10%	51.25	18.38	50.64	1.11	1.16

KEMPTON PARK

Trainer	Wins	Runs	Strike Rate	% Rivals Beaten	P/L	Run To Form %	Impact Value	Market Value
Nicky Henderson	57	242	23.55%	57.33	-36.41	59.09	1.79	2.09
Paul Nicholls	54	254	21.26%	58.44	-40.34	66.14	1.49	1.73
Alan King	20	166	12.05%	53.29	-74.77	58.73	0.96	1.49
Chris Gordon	14	95	14.74%	56.41	-24.15	55.79	1.33	1.27
Dan Skelton	14	126	11.11%	50.36	-31.28	54.37	0.90	1.16
Harry Fry	12	51	23.53%	53.70	1.87	50.00	1.94	1.52
Nigel Twiston-Davies	10	87	11.49%	51.19	-1.75	55.17	0.95	1.13
Ben Pauling	10	55	18.18%	58.18	32.50	68.18	1.58	1.07
Emma Lavelle	10	65	15.38%	56.70	115.80	60.00	1.17	1.17
Fergal O'Brien	9	70	12.86%	57.78	-4.00	59.29	1.12	1.25

LEICESTER

Trainer	Wins	Runs	Strike Rate	% Rivals Beaten	P/L	Run To Form %	Impact Value	Market Value
Dan Skelton	17	51	33.33%	64.44	7.19	71.57	2.19	2.10
Olly Murphy	14	40	35.00%	70.33	41.41	78.75	2.61	1.58
Nigel Twiston-Davies	11	47	23.40%	63.73	17.06	70.21	1.53	1.45
Venetia Williams	9	29	31.03%	71.49	4.82	74.14	2.19	2.40
Philip Hobbs	7	19	36.84%	67.23	3.00	68.42	2.16	2.08
Fergal O'Brien	7	38	18.42%	56.39	-4.43	63.16	1.37	1.87
Tom George	6	32	18.75%	54.65	-3.13	53.13	1.38	1.38
Gary Moore	6	27	22.22%	51.42	-3.08	53.70	1.53	1.45
Kim Bailey	6	28	21.43%	51.46	-4.42	48.21	1.52	1.48
Nicky Henderson	6	20	30.00%	56.45	10.04	52.50	1.51	1.53

LINGFIELD PARK

Trainer	Wins	Runs	Strike Rate	% Rivals Beaten	P/L	Run To Form %	Impact Value	Market Value
Gary Moore	28	146	19.18%	56.93	-0.96	57.19	1.50	1.42
Venetia Williams	10	49	20.41%	66.23	-12.87	72.45	1.61	1.77
Seamus Mullins	8	48	16.67%	51.23	85.88	46.88	1.44	0.89
Olly Murphy	8	35	22.86%	63.45	13.33	68.57	1.84	1.90
Dan Skelton	8	46	17.39%	58.03	-8.78	58.70	1.44	2.04
Nicky Henderson	7	33	21.21%	57.70	-11.39	56.06	1.77	2.34
Chris Gordon	7	51	13.73%	49.60	-22.03	43.14	1.11	1.41
Samuel Drinkwater	6	13	46.15%	72.48	55.25	80.77	3.60	1.20
Lucy Wadham	6	29	20.69%	63.85	26.69	50.00	1.81	1.50
Jamie Snowden	5	25	20.00%	62.47	-4.46	58.00	1.73	1.87

LUDLOW

Trainer	Wins	Runs	Strike Rate	% Rivals Beaten	P/L	Run To Form %	Impact Value	Market Value
Nicky Henderson	25	111	22.52%	60.38	-34.45	68.02	1.66	2.38
Dan Skelton	22	120	18.33%	60.28	-41.84	60.00	1.52	2.19
Kim Bailey	22	97	22.68%	58.18	-1.63	60.82	1.98	2.03
Henry Daly	21	107	19.63%	58.74	-20.75	59.35	1.68	1.46
Philip Hobbs	19	103	18.45%	62.91	-14.68	63.59	1.45	1.87
Paul Nicholls	19	79	24.05%	57.30	-19.73	62.66	1.48	1.96
Fergal O'Brien	18	106	16.98%	60.49	-45.98	62.74	1.26	1.77
Venetia Williams	17	82	20.73%	62.45	7.19	67.07	1.75	1.48
Nigel Twiston-Davies	17	130	13.08%	51.01	-44.74	51.15	1.09	1.36
Evan Williams	16	174	9.20%	47.32	-102.68	48.56	0.67	1.12

MARKET RASEN

Trainer	Wins	Runs	Strike Rate	% Rivals Beaten	P/L	Run To Form %	Impact Value	Market Value
Dan Skelton	54	246	21.95%	60.91	-27.83	61.59	1.67	1.91
Olly Murphy	44	222	19.82%	61.40	-56.93	62.39	1.57	1.74
Fergal O'Brien	27	141	19.15%	59.47	-44.56	63.12	1.40	1.71
Alan King	22	106	20.75%	60.52	-4.23	66.04	1.60	1.72
Dr Richard Newland	20	78	25.64%	65.19	5.26	66.03	2.19	1.99
Nigel Twiston-Davies	16	92	17.39%	51.03	-7.88	55.98	1.40	1.46
Nicky Henderson	16	73	21.92%	54.55	-27.73	60.96	1.63	2.16
Peter Bowen	15	90	16.67%	49.87	11.75	57.78	1.47	1.24
Jonjo O'Neill	14	116	12.07%	48.32	-53.82	53.45	0.99	1.41
Micky Hammond	13	96	13.54%	48.81	4.75	42.71	1.12	0.83

MUSSELBURGH

Trainer	Wins	Runs	Strike Rate	% Rivals Beaten	P/L	Run To Form %	Impact Value	Market Value
Donald McCain	36	164	21.95%	59.98	23.96	63.41	1.58	1.51
Keith Dalgleish	33	164	20.12%	56.95	-9.18	57.62	1.57	1.49
Lucinda Russell	32	274	11.68%	50.32	-70.93	49.45	0.90	1.01
Sandy Thomson	17	84	20.24%	55.71	1.33	59.52	1.53	1.41
Paul Nicholls	17	46	36.96%	66.85	4.84	75.00	2.41	2.29
N. W. Alexander	15	94	15.96%	58.42	-23.50	58.51	1.31	1.32
Iain Jardine	10	141	7.09%	50.89	-90.68	50.71	0.56	1.13
Rose Dobbin	9	55	16.36%	58.37	9.00	66.36	1.39	1.20
L J Morgan	9	21	42.86%	69.44	29.68	61.90	2.95	2.03
Nicky Richards	8	71	11.27%	56.60	-12.50	46.48	1.00	1.42

NEWBURY

Trainer	Wins	Runs	Strike Rate	% Rivals Beaten	P/L	Run To Form %	Impact Value	Market Value
Nicky Henderson	55	253	21.74%	59.28	-20.97	66.21	1.99	2.21
Paul Nicholls	38	165	23.03%	60.80	25.13	67.58	1.79	1.70
Philip Hobbs	19	123	15.45%	57.05	2.79	61.79	1.44	1.42
Fergal O'Brien	14	77	18.18%	59.15	5.33	68.18	1.62	1.74
Alan King	11	166	6.63%	56.02	-103.34	65.06	0.63	1.28
Dan Skelton	10	122	8.20%	48.99	-59.52	52.46	0.77	1.21
David Pipe	10	53	18.87%	60.91	17.83	62.26	2.03	1.28
Gary Moore	10	108	9.26%	46.65	-48.69	49.54	0.89	0.99
Ben Pauling	9	77	11.69%	53.01	-21.63	52.60	1.13	1.27
Nigel Twiston-Davies	8	73	10.96%	52.46	-24.07	51.37	1.04	1.29

NEWCASTLE

Trainer	Wins	Runs	Strike Rate	% Rivals Beaten	P/L	Run To Form %	Impact Value	Market Value
Sue Smith	18	98	18.37%	60.32	-3.89	63.27	1.41	1.46
Donald McCain	17	100	17.00%	53.42	8.47	51.50	1.36	1.58
Rebecca Menzies	16	108	14.81%	57.21	19.99	53.24	1.29	1.27
Nicky Richards	15	96	15.63%	57.53	-22.63	56.77	1.24	1.78
Brian Ellison	14	85	16.47%	55.59	-36.66	56.47	1.28	1.55
Micky Hammond	14	127	11.02%	44.28	-21.86	38.19	0.89	0.96
James Ewart	13	83	15.66%	50.46	-8.50	46.39	1.20	1.23
Sandy Thomson	13	73	17.81%	57.42	97.38	65.07	1.40	1.61
Philip Kirby	13	125	10.40%	47.30	-48.50	42.80	0.91	1.08
Dan Skelton	10	43	23.26%	65.00	-15.35	69.77	2.09	2.35

NEWTON ABBOT

Trainer	Wins	Runs	Strike Rate	% Rivals Beaten	P/L	Run To Form %	Impact Value	Market Value
Paul Nicholls	48	170	28.24%	62.65	-46.95	65.00	1.53	2.01
Fergal O'Brien	22	86	25.58%	68.08	15.38	68.02	2.05	1.99
Philip Hobbs	18	115	15.65%	51.69	-45.99	56.52	1.15	1.64
David Pipe	13	128	10.16%	52.68	-43.92	55.47	0.82	1.31
Harry Fry	13	51	25.49%	64.07	2.19	70.59	1.99	1.92
Dan Skelton	12	78	15.38%	56.46	-39.93	55.77	1.14	2.29
Peter Bowen	12	55	21.82%	51.37	36.01	53.64	1.56	1.12
Nicky Henderson	11	34	32.35%	61.29	1.96	73.53	2.00	1.98
Evan Williams	11	91	12.09%	50.94	-36.40	48.90	0.82	1.25
Emma Lavelle	10	45	22.22%	55.77	8.75	57.78	1.69	1.32

PERTH

Trainer	Wins	Runs	Strike Rate	% Rivals Beaten	P/L	Run To Form %	Impact Value	Market Value
Gordon Elliott, Ireland	48	157	30.57%	65.68	-11.05	68.79	2.13	2.13
Lucinda Russell	32	346	9.25%	47.05	-91.72	44.65	0.73	0.87
Donald McCain	24	83	28.92%	59.32	36.82	65.06	1.90	1.24
Fergal O'Brien	19	72	26.39%	60.05	-1.23	60.42	1.84	1.87
Keith Dalgleish	16	76	21.05%	56.04	8.80	59.87	1.49	1.39
Neil Mulholland	15	63	23.81%	62.13	12.88	63.49	1.92	1.59
Olly Murphy	14	66	21.21%	58.93	15.79	59.85	1.60	1.64
Peter Bowen	14	40	35.00%	62.01	18.37	60.00	2.48	1.76
Nigel Twiston-Davies	13	65	20.00%	55.26	-27.71	56.15	1.36	1.85
Nicky Richards	12	159	7.55%	50.06	-86.61	51.26	0.57	1.37

PLUMPTON

Trainer	Wins	Runs	Strike Rate	% Rivals Beaten	P/L	Run To Form %	Impact Value	Market Value
Gary Moore	51	354	14.41%	51.84	-121.58	55.65	1.03	1.54
Chris Gordon	45	205	21.95%	59.65	-13.45	62.93	1.59	1.61
Seamus Mullins	21	133	15.79%	52.89	5.62	48.87	1.21	0.98
Anthony Honeyball	14	70	20.00%	53.61	-19.59	62.14	1.37	1.95
Neil Mulholland	13	104	12.50%	53.95	-41.85	48.08	0.99	1.12
Alan King	13	56	23.21%	62.88	-20.45	68.75	1.50	2.00
Dan Skelton	12	45	26.67%	62.49	-17.00	63.33	2.08	2.41
Paul Nicholls	12	32	37.50%	65.82	13.86	67.19	2.24	2.20
Sheena West	11	97	11.34%	50.97	12.25	43.81	0.97	1.08
Neil King	10	52	19.23%	48.22	-18.84	47.12	1.24	1.34

SANDOWN PARK

Trainer	Wins	Runs	Strike Rate	% Rivals Beaten	P/L	Run To Form %	Impact Value	Market Value
Nicky Henderson	31	132	23.48%	58.94	-30.26	62.50	1.86	2.04
Gary Moore	23	162	14.20%	46.74	-80.83	48.46	1.10	1.10
Paul Nicholls	22	150	14.67%	54.72	-2.75	64.33	1.15	1.30
Philip Hobbs	16	90	17.78%	55.84	-6.38	58.33	1.52	1.40
Venetia Williams	12	66	18.18%	52.05	-2.01	51.52	1.60	1.57
Nigel Twiston-Davies	11	58	18.97%	51.49	39.80	56.03	1.73	1.39
Fergal O'Brien	7	47	14.89%	53.21	-1.50	57.45	1.42	1.30
Dan Skelton	7	78	8.97%	46.64	-37.75	53.21	0.77	1.15
Alan King	6	50	12.00%	61.21	5.00	75.00	0.97	1.26
Harry Fry	6	39	15.38%	61.00	-20.27	62.82	1.32	1.71

SEDGEFIELD

Trainer	Wins	Runs	Strike Rate	% Rivals Beaten	P/L	Run To Form %	Impact Value	Market Value
Donald McCain	53	269	19.70%	60.78	-8.28	61.15	1.38	1.61
Brian Ellison	38	160	23.75%	60.87	-16.45	64.69	1.60	1.54
Micky Hammond	30	296	10.14%	44.88	-62.68	40.37	0.82	0.95
Sue Smith	25	149	16.78%	53.77	-25.15	55.70	1.28	1.36
Philip Kirby	19	133	14.29%	53.29	-11.29	48.12	1.20	1.23
Rebecca Menzies	17	140	12.14%	52.44	-13.39	53.21	0.96	1.08
Dianne Sayer	16	78	20.51%	56.55	37.46	53.21	1.81	1.34
Sam England	15	96	15.63%	52.31	-22.25	53.65	1.18	1.29
Ben Haslam	13	96	13.54%	50.77	40.73	46.35	1.01	1.02
Jennie Candlish	12	77	15.58%	55.98	-14.13	55.19	1.25	1.40

TRAINERS FOR COURSES

SOUTHWELL

Trainer	Wins	Runs	Strike Rate	% Rivals Beaten	P/L	Run To Form %	Impact Value	Market Value
Dan Skelton	50	222	22.52%	61.99	-57.15	67.57	1.75	2.15
Martin Keighley	25	110	22.73%	59.04	37.98	57.73	1.93	1.28
Jonjo O'Neill	23	133	17.29%	57.58	-23.71	56.77	1.41	1.49
Nicky Henderson	23	68	33.82%	62.74	-3.03	66.91	2.31	2.34
Fergal O'Brien	23	97	23.71%	61.06	11.71	57.73	1.94	1.84
Olly Murphy	19	118	16.10%	57.67	-68.56	55.51	1.34	1.83
Dr Richard Newland	16	60	26.67%	66.65	-9.26	71.67	2.09	2.07
Ben Pauling	15	92	16.30%	53.58	23.51	57.07	1.53	1.57
L J Morgan	13	81	16.05%	44.93	-22.29	38.89	1.31	0.95
Harry Whittington	13	51	25.49%	64.36	10.24	70.59	2.22	1.83

STRATFORD-ON-AVON

Trainer	Wins	Runs	Strike Rate	% Rivals Beaten	P/L	Run To Form %	Impact Value	Market Value
Dan Skelton	38	160	23.75%	61.49	-42.76	63.13	1.82	2.21
Dr Richard Newland	18	75	24.00%	60.63	-28.31	61.33	1.60	1.96
Nigel Twiston-Davies	17	83	20.48%	57.91	1.03	60.84	1.57	1.44
Fergal O'Brien	17	100	17.00%	57.14	-21.44	53.50	1.33	1.85
Olly Murphy	16	118	13.56%	49.73	-62.54	51.69	1.11	1.53
Donald McCain	14	64	21.88%	61.23	2.10	57.81	1.61	1.35
Jonjo O'Neill	13	87	14.94%	49.99	2.73	50.57	1.23	1.27
Charlie Longsdon	13	66	19.70%	59.11	10.03	64.39	1.55	1.26
Paul Nicholls	12	36	33.33%	70.22	1.68	72.22	2.29	2.49
Nicky Henderson	12	38	31.58%	63.48	0.57	56.58	2.14	1.84

TAUNTON

Trainer	Wins	Runs	Strike Rate	% Rivals Beaten	P/L	Run To Form %	Impact Value	Market Value
Paul Nicholls	51	185	27.57%	68.86	-25.35	70.54	2.25	2.67
Philip Hobbs	27	155	17.42%	65.82	-32.49	69.03	1.64	1.65
Nigel Hawke	14	109	12.84%	52.40	-23.75	49.54	1.37	1.11
Jeremy Scott	14	83	16.87%	58.44	23.48	59.04	1.71	1.63
Neil Mulholland	14	105	13.33%	50.93	-13.69	42.38	1.26	1.07
David Pipe	12	140	8.57%	50.74	-63.33	46.43	0.85	1.20
Evan Williams	11	126	8.73%	48.22	-61.63	44.84	0.75	0.97
Harry Fry	10	73	13.70%	59.58	-34.68	58.90	1.31	2.05
Olly Murphy	10	54	18.52%	62.47	-26.74	64.81	1.74	1.77
Nicky Henderson	9	38	23.68%	63.27	-3.67	71.05	1.88	1.79

UTTOXETER

Trainer	Wins	Runs	Strike Rate	% Rivals Beaten	P/L	Run To Form %	Impact Value	Market Value
Dan Skelton	89	331	26.89%	64.21	6.16	63.75	2.36	2.19
Dr Richard Newland	29	112	25.89%	67.27	-7.75	64.73	2.09	2.23
Jonjo O'Neill	28	210	13.33%	49.85	-13.30	49.76	1.18	1.39
Olly Murphy	26	138	18.84%	60.17	-15.13	56.88	1.61	1.76
Fergal O'Brien	23	151	15.23%	58.81	-24.78	62.25	1.25	1.69
Nicky Henderson	22	86	25.58%	60.88	-17.81	54.65	2.00	2.30
Harry Fry	21	75	28.00%	58.79	21.83	64.00	2.39	1.98
Charlie Longsdon	17	101	16.83%	55.39	-9.38	56.44	1.47	1.33
Neil Mulholland	17	141	12.06%	47.56	-34.16	48.23	1.09	1.16
Donald McCain	15	115	13.04%	50.32	-18.18	48.26	1.11	0.94

WARWICK

Trainer	Wins	Runs	Strike Rate	% Rivals Beaten	P/L	Run To Form %	Impact Value	Market Value
Dan Skelton	64	287	22.30%	59.55	-45.18	63.94	1.84	2.00
Nicky Henderson	35	134	26.12%	66.84	7.88	69.03	2.23	2.56
Alan King	33	150	22.00%	64.37	-35.76	63.67	1.95	1.96
Jonjo O'Neill	31	171	18.13%	53.49	65.36	55.26	1.60	1.34
Philip Hobbs	18	122	14.75%	57.20	-33.92	56.56	1.29	1.61
Nigel Twiston-Davies	16	164	9.76%	52.39	-94.31	52.13	0.83	1.26
Kim Bailey	15	76	19.74%	60.23	12.63	58.55	1.96	1.54
Fergal O'Brien	13	97	13.40%	55.73	-36.90	60.31	1.15	1.57
Paul Nicholls	12	44	27.27%	63.07	-12.87	72.73	1.57	1.88
Lucy Wadham	11	62	17.74%	63.58	61.95	60.48	1.53	1.42

WETHERBY

Trainer	Wins	Runs	Strike Rate	% Rivals Beaten	P/L	Run To Form %	Impact Value	Market Value
Dan Skelton	48	169	28.40%	66.62	-2.29	71.30	2.14	2.16
Philip Kirby	23	181	12.71%	46.57	-42.71	46.69	1.15	0.96
Micky Hammond	23	287	8.01%	44.45	37.88	42.68	0.69	0.69
Nigel Twiston-Davies	15	82	18.29%	55.73	-24.00	57.32	1.43	1.66
Jonjo O'Neill	15	72	20.83%	59.90	-8.58	60.42	1.78	1.72
Donald McCain	11	106	10.38%	51.42	-47.94	50.47	0.83	1.29
Rebecca Menzies	11	64	17.19%	52.87	7.88	55.47	1.46	0.96
Fergal O'Brien	11	54	20.37%	60.93	-5.91	60.19	1.70	2.47
Kim Bailey	10	55	18.18%	58.35	-28.13	60.00	1.40	2.04
Charlie Longsdon	10	48	20.83%	61.50	-3.73	61.46	1.54	1.55

WINCANTON

Trainer	Wins	Runs	Strike Rate	% Rivals Beaten	P/L	Run To Form %	Impact Value	Market Value
Paul Nicholls	81	303	26.73%	64.45	-43.03	68.81	1.99	2.64
Philip Hobbs	24	197	12.18%	54.99	-46.00	58.12	1.12	1.24
Jeremy Scott	20	128	15.63%	55.20	102.05	51.56	1.44	1.25
Neil Mulholland	13	158	8.23%	53.83	-49.90	49.05	0.77	1.01
Chris Gordon	12	47	25.53%	60.21	40.83	61.70	2.34	1.29
Emma Lavelle	12	72	16.67%	60.51	2.80	61.11	1.57	1.50
Harry Fry	12	79	15.19%	56.18	-13.84	57.59	1.39	1.80
Robert Walford	10	71	14.08%	53.55	-1.75	47.18	1.30	1.20
Alan King	10	96	10.42%	56.48	-55.27	58.85	0.87	1.49
Anthony Honeyball	9	63	14.29%	56.87	18.50	50.79	1.26	1.30

WORCESTER

Trainer	Wins	Runs	Strike Rate	% Rivals Beaten	P/L	Run To Form %	Impact Value	Market Value
Dr Richard Newland	30	113	26.55%	66.56	4.00	69.91	2.04	2.14
Jonjo O'Neill	27	158	17.09%	57.18	-41.06	56.96	1.39	1.53
Philip Hobbs	27	94	28.72%	60.27	69.52	56.91	2.22	1.81
Dan Skelton	26	151	17.22%	58.59	-35.49	57.95	1.42	1.89
Nicky Henderson	22	84	26.19%	61.65	15.51	64.88	1.90	2.02
Fergal O'Brien	21	117	17.95%	59.85	5.56	59.40	1.44	1.67
Peter Bowen	17	99	17.17%	55.28	41.33	55.56	1.48	1.37
Paul Nicholls	15	45	33.33%	65.64	9.01	67.78	2.05	2.13
Nigel Twiston-Davies	15	79	18.99%	55.62	-22.44	53.80	1.57	1.41
Neil Mulholland	15	158	9.49%	49.28	-65.89	52.85	0.80	1.13

TOP DOGS

Get daily news and expert analysis from Timeform for all the major UK daytime and evening action, including best bets, star ratings and 1-2-3 verdicts

Cards • Tips • Form • Results

Play smarter at
timeform.com/greyhound-racing

TIMEFORM
GREYHOUNDS

Index To Photographers

	Photographer	Page
Ahoy Senor looks a top-class staying chaser in the making	Bill Selwyn	5
Aucunrisque (black cap) won four of his six starts over hurdles last season	Bill Selwyn	6
Complete Unknown showed improved form to get off the mark at Sandown	Bill Selwyn	12
Gelino Bello (left) should take high rank as a staying novice chaser	Bill Selwyn	18
Jonbon jumps the last on his way to victory at Ascot	Bill Selwyn	25
North Lodge edges to the front at Cheltenham	Bill Selwyn	36
Skytastic (right) has the physique to take well to chasing	Bill Selwyn	43
Unexpected Party is clear of his rivals at Ascot	Bill Selwyn	49
Patrick Mullins celebrates after guiding Ashroe Diamond to victory at Aintree	Bill Selwyn	55
El Fabiolo (left) is locked in battle with Jonbon at Aintree	Bill Selwyn	58
Fil Dor (red cap) found only Vauban (pink) too good at Cheltenham	Bill Selwyn	61
All roads lead to the Champion Hurdle for Constitution Hill	Bill Selwyn	79
Sporting John (right) could develop into a key contender for the Stayers' Hurdle	Bill Selwyn	81
L'Homme Presse should relish the Gold Cup trip	Bill Selwyn	82
A Plus Tard begins to pull clear of Minella Indo in the Gold Cup	Bill Selwyn	107
Energumene (right) leads Shishkin over the last at Ascot	Bill Selwyn	108
Honeysuckle is now unbeaten in 16 starts under Rules	Bill Selwyn	111